Planning and Using Time in the Foundation Stage

Also available:

Developing Early Years Practice
Linda Miller, Carrie Cable and Jane Devereux
1 84312 317 7

Working with Children in the Early Years
Jane Devereux and Linda Miller
1 85346 975 0

Planning Children's Play and Learning in the Foundation Stage (2nd edn)
Jane Drake
1 84312 151 4

Essential Skills for Managers of Child-Centred Settings
Emma Isles-Buck and Shelly Newstead
1 84312 034 8

Key Persons in the Nursery
Building Relationships for Quality Provision
Peter Elfer, Elinor Goldschmied and Dorothy Selleck
1 84312 079 8

Planning an Appropriate Curriculum for the Under Fives (2nd edn)
A Guide for Students, Teachers and Assistants
Rosemary Rodger
1 85346 912 2

Planning the Pre-5 Setting
Practical Ideas and Activities for the Nursery
Christine Macintyre and Kim McVitty
1 84312 058 5

Organising Play in the Early Years
Practical Ideas for Practitioners
Jane Drake
1 84312 025 9

Planning and Using Time in the Foundation Stage

Jill Williams and Karen McInnes

David Fulton Publishers

To all the early years pioneers and inspirational educators whose work has been overlooked in our haste for children to meet deadlines and hit targets.

David Fulton Publishers Ltd
The Chiswick Centre, 414 Chiswick High Road, London W4 5TF

www.fultonpublishers.co.uk

David Fulton Publishers is a division of Granada Learning Limited, part of ITV plc.

British Library Cataloguing in Publication Data
A catalogue record for this book is available from the British Library.

ISBN: 1 84312 279 0

10 9 8 7 6 5 4 3 2 1

Typeset by RefineCatch Limited, Bungay, Suffolk
Printed and bound in Great Britain

Contents

Acknowledgements

There are many people we would like to thank for giving us their time in order to engage in reflection and discussion concerning early years practice. We also need to thank people who have allowed us the time and space to write.

First, we would like to thank Kieron P. Griffin (Mrs H. M. Davies Will Trust) for allowing us to use the poem 'Leisure', written by William Henry Davies, which contains pertinent sentiments in relation to time and how we use it.

We would like to thank all the staff at the Limes Nursery School in Bristol for sharing their knowledge, understanding and exemplary early years practice. We would like to thank the staff in the Foundation Stage at Broomhill Infants School in Bristol for sharing their practice and for the pleasure of engaging in fruitful and thoughtful discussion concerning early years practice and what is right for young children. We would also like to thank Ed Harker, Nursery Teacher and Foundation Stage Co-ordinator at St Saviour's Infants School in Bath, for informative conversations and inspiring practice.

We would like to thank all the students, teachers and children we have worked with over the years who have challenged us and made us reflect upon and question what we do, and to Charlotte Rogers, early years technician at Bath Spa University College, who saved us from our technical ineptitude. Finally, we need to thank our families: Reg has lived through several publications and has come through smiling. Colin, Sophie and Millie have given support, love and hugs that have helped to see the book to its conclusion. We also need to thank Sophie and Millie for all the little stories and anecdotes that have kept us laughing while writing!

Preface

In our work with early years teachers and students we have often heard the refrain 'but we haven't got enough time . . .' in relation to observation, responding to the needs of individual children, discussing practice with colleagues, taking part in further training and all the other activities that ensure high quality practice and experiences for young children. It is true that time is an issue that affects society as a whole, not just early years practitioners. There are those who would say that as shortage of time is a life issue, why write a book about it? We have felt compelled to write this book because we believe practitioners can do something about how they use time with children, and we know of practitioners who have done just that.

This book is intended as a resource for colleagues who feel rushed in their work with children and as a useful support for those training to be early years practitioners who can reflect on the use of time with young children while they have the time to do so. In this book we have drawn upon theory and practice to reflect on how time is used in early years practice. We have tried to raise questions and make suggestions that will enable practitioners to reflect on the issue of how time is used with young children. Ultimately, we hope that practitioners and children are enabled to have time, as W.H. Davies says, to 'stand and stare'.

LEISURE

What is this life if, full of care,
We have no time to stand and stare.

No time to stand beneath the boughs
And stare as long as sheep and cows.

No time to see, when woods we pass,
Where squirrels hide their nuts in grass.

No time to see, in broad daylight,
Streams full of stars, like skies at night.

No time to turn at Beauty's glance,
And watch her feet, how they can dance.

No time to wait till her mouth can
Enrich that smile her eyes began.

A poor life this if, full of care,
We have no time to stand and stare.

(Williams Henry Davies 1871–1940, BBC 1996)

Introduction

No time to wait till her mouth can
Enrich that smile her eyes began.

(W.H. Davies)

There are a number of reasons why slow knowing has fallen into disuse. Partly it is due to our changing conception of, and attitude towards, time. In pre-seventeenth-century Europe a leisurely approach to thinking was much more common, and in other cultures it still is. A tribal meeting at a Maori *marae* can last for days, until everyone has had time to assimilate the issues, to have their say, and to form a consensus. However, the idea that time is plentiful is in many parts of the world now seen as laughably old-fashioned and self-indulgent.

(Claxton 1998: 4)

Why have we come to accept that time as a resource is both precious and yet contested? We have allowed the demands of work, family, and keeping up with the exigencies of society to combine and make us feel as if we are constantly trying to catch up with ourselves. We feel guilty if we take time to reflect on situations, to make sense of new experiences or simply to 'stand and stare'. If adults find *time* hard to handle, then how much more difficult it is for children to take the time they need to communicate, to interact, to explore, observe and listen. Children need adults who are sensitive to their curiosity, can sustain interest, offer ideas, intervene appropriately and 'elicit children's thoughtful participation' (DES 1990: 11). The current framework for the early years curriculum (QCA 2000: 11) qualifies this by saying that: 'Children need time to become engrossed, work in depth and complete activities.' Surely, then, the 'slow knowing' that Claxton is talking about should be the prerogative of young children?

The seeds for this book were sown many years ago when both authors reflected on the rapid pace of change that was taking place in education as a whole and the vulnerability of non-statutory early education. There was an alarming shift in practitioners' attitudes towards time. They seemed to be under increasing pressure to satisfy an outcome-driven early years experience. What children had achieved was more important than the children themselves and their approach to learning. Are the principles for early education, stated in *The Curriculum Guidance for the Foundation Stage* (QCA 2000: 11–12), simply idealistic? Is the reality of their implementation often articulated more like this?

> 'There is never enough time . . . if only we could spend more time . . . if I had time I would . . . that's all very well but we don't have time . . . we have to produce evidence so there is no time to . . .!' 'It's good to observe but we need to be working with the children all the time.' (overheard while working with practitioners)

It has always been a privilege to work with practitioners and to listen to their hopes, aspirations and concerns for the education of young children. On many evenings, when they had completed a day in school, we shared exciting and innovative practice, reflected on the true potential of children and talked about taking risks and pushing out boundaries. It seemed to us, however, that current pressures were eroding the time that should be spent on understanding children's development and making provision for them to satisfy their curiosity and develop their interests, skills and understanding. How easy it is to reminisce and to reflect on a system that was seemingly better than the current one. Throughout the book we talk about the pockets of excellent practice, in early years education, in previous decades. We are realistic, however, in recognising that there was inequality in availability and quality of provision.

The Rumbold Report (DES 1990) had provided a sound framework for the early years curriculum. It described the range of learning areas that should form a framework for the curriculum and recognised the time that children need to develop. It provided a rationale for early education and gave practitioners important, written evidence of the good practice that many of them had carried out but never articulated. The report was written in response to the rapid changes in education but was, however, largely ignored. It was published in the shadow of the National Curriculum. Provision for early years education continued in an *ad hoc* manner with patches of excellence and furrows of indifferent practice. The opportunities for children below statutory school age were clearly unequal.

The Early Learning Goals, published in 1999, had their foundation in the Rumbold Report. They provided a clear set of outcomes for children's learning but were published initially without a framework to support their implementation. The subsequent *Curriculum Guidance for the Foundation Stage* (QCA 2000) became statutory in all settings, including reception classes in primary schools. In spite of the very clear importance of children's development voiced in the framework and the message that the use of *time* must be appropriate to the age and stage of the children, there were problems from the outset.

In this book we question and challenge the use of time with young children. We pose questions and recognise that some of them have been answered and others are left unanswered. Finding unanswered questions in a text can cause irritation. There are, however, two reasons for leaving questions unanswered. First, there may be no quick answer as the question posed will probably need to be related to a particular setting. Second, questions may well be used to provoke discussion among practitioners and provide material for reviewing and analysing practice in settings.

The succession of themes covered by the chapters provides a journey of discovery that starts with the recognition that *time* should be valued and that effective use of *time* makes a contribution to learning. We stress the need for *time* to look, listen, record and assess learning. A true partnership with parents is not a feature of all early years settings. If such a partnership is to be achieved, *time* needs to be taken to allow exchange of ideas and expertise and to value opinions. Time for genuine dialogue is time well invested. Throughout the book there is reference to the Reggio Emilia approach to early education. This is an educational system where the role of parents and the wider community formed the basis for its development and is a continuous part of its daily process. The next theme to be addressed is how to manage *time*. The questions posed in this chapter are intended to be used by practitioners in the context of their settings. The final chapter provides practical ideas for auditing the use of *time*. The whole text provides theoretical, reflective and practical material that gives practitioners the opportunity to consider their work as a team and to make relevant and informed changes. The questions that remain unanswered or that still cause concern, as well as questions that arise from discussion, should be returned to as a part of the development of programmes in individual settings.

Any system for early years education needs to reflect the changing needs of society and the requirements for young children to become responsible citizens of the future. Although early years practitioners require openness to innovation and reflection on modification of practice, they need to hang on to a philosophy and pedagogy that celebrates the unique potential of children. Along with the willingness to adapt to changing views must always be the belief that it takes *time* to understand children and *time* to give them a holistic view of the world.

Anybody who has worked with young children will understand that learning can be a two-way process. Adults and children have differing views of the world. The adult has been conditioned: excited and possibly disillusioned. The young child looks at the world with new eyes. When the adult supports the child, they share the experience and help one another to make sense of what they see. This takes time. In the chapters that follow we attempt to unravel the problems of time and the way that we manage time with young children. Valuing time and understanding why time should be used effectively are important for the well-being of both children and adults.

CHAPTER 1

How do we recognise and value time with children?

Aside from sleeping, and perhaps playing, there is no other activity that occupies as much of the child's time as that involved in attending school. Apart from the bedroom (where he has his eyes closed most of the time) there is no single enclosure in which he spends a longer time than in the classroom.

(Jackson 1968, cited in Alexander 2000)

The purpose of our book is to consider how time can be used effectively in whatever situation or setting the child may find himself. The current pattern of early education in England with its variety of provision has seemingly inevitable anomalies in the use of time. We explore some of the important influences on the education of young children and consider how these influences affect the quality of the use of time in the Foundation Stage. Children's experience of time, space and the opportunity to make relationships will help to shape the people that they will become. The organisation of these aspects of the curriculum will depend on how the adults in the setting view children's development and the importance that they place on provision that supports young children's learning. It will further depend on the trust that adults place in young children and the confidence that adults have in standing by the principles set out in the *Curriculum Guidance for the Foundation Stage* (QCA 2000: 11).

Children spend long periods of their day in a variety of settings. According to a survey in 2004 (BBC 13 July 2004), they may have experienced four different cultures before reaching Key Stage 1 (e.g. home, playgroup, nursery, reception class). It was reported that there were inconsistencies between the various settings in the use of time, space and opportunities for active learning. Children, particularly in reception classes, spent too long sitting still on the 'carpet', had little time to play and were denied free access to outdoor play. Creative and expressive communication was also not developed (Ofsted 2004a). This paints a dismal picture of the implementation of the curriculum guidance but fortuitously provides straightforward evidence to support the explorations in the following chapters.

Inconsistencies in the nature of provision for young children are the result of a combination of factors. Among these will be the different training programmes that practitioners have undertaken. They may have been presented with differing views of the needs of young children and of how learning can be supported effectively. This will result in different ideas on pedagogy or the way in which they teach and similarly different views on the way that children learn. Examples to illustrate this include teachers who are trained to teach Key Stage 2 and then teach in a reception class with no further training, teachers who have been trained to teach in the Foundation Stage but have had no child development included in their training, and teachers who have had curricular elements omitted from their training, such as history or dance, and do not have sufficient understanding of the need for breadth and depth in the curriculum.

Children and time in the Foundation Stage

In September 2000 the Foundation Stage, in England, was introduced. This was to be a continuous stage of educational experience for all children from the age of three to the end of the reception year. *The Curriculum Guidance for the Foundation Stage* (QCA 2000) provides a framework within which practitioners can work and sets out the early learning goals for young children. The goals are reached by a series of stepping stones and it is the responsibility of the practitioner to provide appropriate experiences to ensure that children are able to achieve them. In the framework there is emphasis on children being active, organising their own learning experiences, using talk and interacting with others. It is seen as important that the curriculum should be planned with opportunities for play to support exploration, control, risk taking and problem solving. These are positive aims and have important implications for young children as learners. It leaves us with the message that in order to deliver a curriculum that will satisfy the needs of growing minds, 'practitioners must understand the stages of learning through which young children pass' and 'the characteristics of young children as learners' (Drake 2001: vi). The more we understand about young children, the more we will appreciate the way that time can be used most effectively with them. We are very fortunate that the Foundation Stage has a set of guidelines underpinned by sound principles.

All children from three years to the end of the reception year are in the Foundation Stage. This may seem like repetition but it is an important statement. What age, then, do children start school? What are the reasons for the timing? What difference will it make to individuals? Many practitioners working with young children ask these questions privately but have to accept the situation and plan for it accordingly. If they feel that there is an erosion of children's rights through the timing being wrong and the situation inappropriate, they feel ill equipped to argue. This should never be the case and as practitioners working with young children we should always question, reflect and argue for what we believe is right for children's well-being.

Time to start school

The statutory age at which children start school is the term after a child's fifth birthday (Woodhead 1989). This is earlier than in other countries with six or seven years of age being the norm in Europe and the rest of the world (Sharp 2002). However, is this the reality for all children? In fact, the school starting age is earlier still with four years of age being the norm due to the practice of admitting children into the reception class at the beginning of the year in which they become five. There are a number of reasons for this. In the 1970s and early 1980s falling primary school rolls meant that there was spare classroom space which needed to be filled with young children to keep up the school numbers and to maintain teachers' jobs. Then the introduction of the nursery voucher scheme (SCAA 1996) accelerated this trend further as head teachers realised that four-year-olds would bring much needed voucher funding with them (Pugh 1996).

Another change in admission policy was due to the concern over the perceived disadvantage to summer-born children. These children had traditionally received less infant schooling than other children in the same year group. Therefore, to counter this, it was deemed more beneficial for them to start in the autumn term of the academic year in which they became five and have three terms' schooling (Ofsted 1993) despite there being a scanty evidence base for this decision. Currently there is the additional pressure on children having to achieve the early learning goals by the end of the reception year. As a consequence those local authorities that had maintained a two- or three-term entry are moving to a one-term entry to allow children more chance to achieve the learning goals (Ofsted 2004a).

All of these changes result in a nominal school starting age of four years old and at present 61 per cent of all four-year-olds, including summer-born children, are in infant classes in primary schools (DfES 2004). This is in spite of concerns voiced by practitioners and parents (McInnes 2001).

It can be argued, however, that the age at which our children start school is, in reality, earlier still – three years of age. The Sure Start unit, established to implement the national early years agenda and coordinate early years services (DfES/DWP 2002), states that there is now a free part-time education place for all three- and four-year-olds whose parents want it (Sure Start 2004). At present there are 93 per cent of three-year-olds taking up free part-time early years places (DfES 2004). Also as the Foundation Stage begins at age three, children from three years of age may be in educational and care settings such as playgroups, childminders, nursery classes, and early excellence centres. They will be receiving educational experiences framed around a statutory curriculum despite what practitioners and parents may want for their children. So having ascertained when children start school and why they start school at such a young age, we must ask, do we use children's time to their best advantage and is this acceptable and appropriate?

Many would argue that experiences for children are appropriate in terms of the environment, activities and adult interactions. This, however, is a position that can be argued and debated from a variety of moral, philosophical and educational stances. In this book we reflect on some of these influences within the context of how time is valued and used with young children.

Influences on our use of time

There are a variety of theoretical and practical influences that determine how we use time with young children. These will be determined further by:

- the type of setting;
- the pedagogy or teaching style;
- theories of learning.

The type of setting

During the course of a day children in the Foundation Stage may spend their time in one or many settings (QCA 2000). These include:

- a playgroup;
- a childminder's home;
- a nursery class;
- a nursery school or combined centre;
- a reception class.

These different settings have potentially different working practices and philosophies that impact on how their practitioners use time with children. This is the focus for the section that follows. For a more comprehensive overview of provision for the care and education of young children, see Devereux and Miller (2003).

A playgroup

Practitioners working in a playgroup may have constraints upon their time such as having to set up and put away all equipment at the beginning and end of sessions and this will limit the amount of time they have to spend with young children and influence what they put out and how it is organised. This, in turn, will impact on the time children have to use equipment and how they use it. There may not be an outdoor area so children will not have time to work outside. The adults working with the children will have different levels of training, experience and views of how to work with children and this will inevitably affect how time is used with children in the setting.

A childminder's home

Childminders work with young children in their own homes and as a consequence there can be, and usually is, greater fluidity in how time is used with children. Time is less compartmentalised and often time is taken to follow children's interests. Routines of the day such as snack time and lunchtime are often taken when the children are ready and children can often take a nap when they feel they need one. Children are also more often taken on outings such as the local park, shopping or local places of interest where they can spend a good length of time on one activity or activities that are linked.

A nursery class

Time in a nursery class is often more compartmentalised than in the previous settings. Timetables, which are part of a whole school ethos, are often used and strictly followed. There are usually the demands of the rest of the school to take into account such as organisation of play-times and use of the school hall which impact on the daily routine offered to the children. There are also the views of other colleagues to contend with, as well as demands from the head teacher, which may differ or even conflict with how time might be best used with children. A common issue often causing conflict is the time children spend engaged in playful learning.

A nursery school or combined centre

A nursery school or combined centre is usually a setting where all practitioners are trained to work with young children and are focused on their needs. The day is usually organised according to timetables but there is usually opportunity for time to be used in different ways. Practitioners in these settings tend to escape the downward pressures faced by their colleagues in nursery classes but still have to contend with the demands of the local education authority and Ofsted. However, as more centres offer extended hours with *wrap around care*, there may be pressure on how time is used. How do you use time effectively when children start and end at different times? How do you manage time to provide care and education, and can these be separated? These are issues that more settings are having to address.

A reception class

Time and how it is used with young children are subject to many pressures in the reception class. Recent research (Bell and Finch 2004) concludes that the basic length of the school day is too long for children and that they cannot cope. Many of the issues confronted by practitioners in the nursery class are the same for practitioners in the reception class. However, there are additional demands centred around having to accommodate the requirements for literacy and numeracy, and in particular the literacy and numeracy hours, and deal with parents who take a close interest in how time is being used to teach their children now they are in school.

These different settings are subject to scrutiny and *The Effective Provision of Pre-School Education (EPPE) Project* (Sylva *et al.* 1997–2003) assessed the quality of provision across different types of early years settings. The measures used to assess quality included looking at how time is used in the setting through organisation and routines. Evidence from the project suggests that settings vary in quality, with nursery schools combining care and education, including early excellence centres, faring best of all. That, however, does not necessarily mean that time is used effectively with children.

The pedagogy or teaching style

How we teach is a combination of many factors and these include:

- the training we receive;
- our view of children;
- the age of the children with whom we work;
- our understanding of how children learn;
- our experiences of working with children;
- any further training we may have received.

Each of these factors needs to be unpicked so that we can understand what makes us the practitioners we are and how this influences our use of time with children.

Training

All practitioners working in the Foundation Stage will have received some training in working with young children which may vary from day courses to much longer ones. Training in the early years will vary in emphasis between the care and education of young children, with some practitioners receiving more input on care while for others the emphasis will have been on education. There is the potential argument that those who have received more in-depth training on care and the personal, social and emotional development of children will be better placed to recognise and respond to their time-based needs, for example, recognising and responding to children when they need time to reflect and ponder on an activity or when they need time to be reassured and made to feel secure.

Early years teachers may have undertaken a four-year BEd degree, possibly specialising in the Foundation Stage. They may have a first degree in a subject related to education and have completed a one-year postgraduate qualification with a specialist focus on early years education. On the other hand, the degree subject may be unrelated to education and the one-year postgraduate qualification may be more general. Teachers completing qualifications in different institutions, while all meeting the standards set down by the Teacher Training Agency (DfES/TTA 2002), will have had different emphases. However, despite the different training routes, how many teachers will have had the opportunity to consider the importance of time for young children?

Findings from the EPPE Project (Sylva *et al.* 1997–2003) highlight the fact that the more highly qualified the practitioners working in early years settings are, the better the quality of the provision: 'Settings that have staff with higher qualifications have higher quality scores and their children make more progress' (Sylva *et al.* 2004: 1). However, certainly among teachers working in early years settings, many are not initially trained to teach the 3–8 age phase (Blenkin and Yue 1994) and are therefore not relevantly trained and will not necessarily understand the needs of young children. The way in which we have been trained and the chosen content and style of delivery will heavily influence our understanding of young children and consequently how we use time for ourselves and for children.

How we view children

It is worth reflecting on how we view children and childhood because this will have an impact on how we understand and make use of our training and how we use time with children. Views of childhood have evolved over many years and will vary according to certain cultural determinants: historical, social, including social class, political, economic and geographic (for a detailed discussion of historical views, see Boushel *et al.* 2000). The brief discussion that follows shows something of the complexity of these views and serves to remind us of the influence that some of these views have had on current thinking.

In 1693, John Locke put forward the view that the child was a *tabula rasa* or blank slate and as such it was the responsibility of the adult to provide knowledge. In 1762, Rousseau, the Swiss philosopher, wrote about the fictitious child, Emile. He presented a view of children as being innocent until corrupted by society. He advocated natural ways of child rearing where children had freedom and time to play. In 1799, Hannah More, an opponent of rights for women, suggested that children were not innocent, they needed their will broken and should be educated to rectify their corrupt natures. In the 1800s the Romantic view of childhood was shown in painting and poetry with poets such as Wordsworth and Blake portraying children as innocent and beautiful.

In the 1800s the middle-class Victorian home was seen as a haven, with the mother managing servants and in charge of housekeeping and child rearing. In these circumstances, time was given to childhood and children. On the other hand, the reality of lower-class children's life was often precarious with risk of disease, poor diet and early death. Charles Dickens was one author who provided powerful descriptions of the exploitation of children. At this time there was an explosion of evangelical tracts and children's literature concerned with right and wrong and moral well-being. As a result of the Industrial Revolution, an apprenticeship model of childhood developed with the industrial concept of transmission of knowledge and skills. Children were compared to slaves. Reform movements developed as a result of concern over the experiences of many children and institutions such as Dr Barnardo's and the National Children's Home were established to combat deprivation and disease.

By the end of the 1800s children as young as two years attended state schools because of a lack of childcare and the need for women to work in industry. The learning was by rote and there was no opportunity for practical experience. By the turn of the last century schooling for children under seven years had become established in the poorer areas under the influence of pioneers such as Margaret McMillan in London and Maria Montessori in Italy. There was an insistence that children thrived in special environments.

The age of the children with whom we work

Should the age of the children with whom we work impact significantly on our practice and use of time? Three-, four- and five-year-old children are young and there can be vast differences in skills, knowledge and understanding between these age groups, yet they all learn in the same way as outlined above. *The Curriculum Guidance for the Foundation Stage* (QCA 2000) identifies stepping stones for the six areas of learning which chart a progression in skills, knowledge, understanding and attitudes through which children need to progress to achieve the early learning goals at the end of the Foundation Stage. However, the guidance clearly states that 'they are not age related' (ibid.: 5).

A special case has traditionally been put forward for four-year-olds (Cleave and Brown 1991; Dowling 1995) who both argue that four-year-olds have distinct needs and should be treated differently. However, this has been argued in the context of four-year-olds being admitted to formally run reception classes delivering the National Curriculum. It can be argued that it is the content that should differ for three-, four- and five-year-olds, not the practice, as with the introduction of the Foundation Stage teaching should follow the principles and guidelines laid out in the curriculum guidance. However, perceived pressures and constraints on time may mean that this does not actually happen in practice. All young children need time to learn and time should be managed sensitively to accommodate their needs.

Understanding how children learn

The training we receive as budding practitioners should include elements of child development, including how children learn. However, this is not always the case. Teachers who have been trained to teach in the Foundation Stage should have received some input in this important area although it may be cursory. Teachers who have not been trained to teach this age group will most likely not have received this element in their studies. Our understanding of how children learn is derived from the work of theorists such as Piaget, Vygotsky and Bruner and will be discussed later in the chapter.

Children learn through:

- being active and engaging in first-hand experiences;
- using language;
- working with others;
- engaging in meaningful activities;
- feeling secure and experiencing success;
- organising their own learning experiences;
- appropriate adult intervention.

(adapted from Dowling 1992 and Fisher 2002a)

Knowledge and understanding of these elements should inform our work. Children need time and space to be active and they need time to use language in a variety of ways and with others. Recent research by Siraj-Blatchford *et al.* (2002) shows the importance of adults and children engaging in interactions which involve 'sustained shared thinking'. How often do children have time to share in sustained, in-depth interactions? Time has to be organised so that children can engage in child-initiated activities as well as those we wish them to complete. Finally, we need to organise our own time effectively so that we can intervene in children's learning appropriately, in-depth and in a meaningful way. As stated in the curriculum guidance, practitioners need to 'plan their time well so that most of it is spent working directly with children' (QCA 2000: 16).

Our experiences of working with children

During the course of our working lives we hopefully gain many different experiences of interacting with children in different settings. This enables us to see different ways of working and certainly different ways of organising and managing time to work with children. Different types of settings have different constraints and influences on their working practice. In the course of the development of early years education in this country the ways of working with children have changed. Figures 1.1, 1.2 and 1.3 are all of experiences of four-year-old children. The first photograph (Figure 1.1), taken in the 1960s, shows children being given time to work independently and to follow through their ideas. In the second photograph (Figure 1.2), taken in the 1980s, the workspace has been organised according to the principles of the High/Scope curriculum and children are working independently within an adult-directed framework. The third photograph (Figure 1.3) illustrates a structure imposed from central government. No longer are the children given independence and the framework is predetermined. Changes are inevitable but what would appear to be unfortunate, however, is that the changes can bring about a shift in belief and a shaking of the foundations of our understanding of what is important for children's learning.

Figure 1.1   Four-year-olds engaged in serious endeavour in the 1960s

Figure 1.2   Four-year-olds working independently within the High/Scope framework

Figure 1.3   Children engaged in the Literacy Hour

The different settings will also have practitioners working in them who will hold diverse views of children and again this will impact on the practice within the setting. Moving around settings will allow us to view, discuss and debate and consequently clarify our own views and practice, hopefully for the well-being of the children.

Further training

Many practitioners will argue that they do not have time in their busy working lives to engage in further training. However, practitioners should continually reflect on their practice and seek out ways to further their own professional development, as this will benefit them as practitioners and also benefit the children with whom they work. This may involve attending courses within the local education authority, attending local and national conferences related to areas of interest or attending courses at higher education institutions, leading to the award of further qualifications. All these options do take time but it is time well spent. Whichever of these routes are taken, and it could be a combination of all of them, it allows us the opportunity to reflect on our practice and make appropriate changes which will lead to increased quality provision in the setting.

Theories of learning that have affected early education

Early years education has a long and rich tradition and has been shaped over time by theories of learning. These theories have implications for the use of time. These and other philosophical, sociological and psychological theories have been drawn on to support a range of educational frameworks for early education. The issue of how young children learn has been debated for centuries and written about by philosophers, psychologists and educationalists. Historical theories have inevitably shaped our thinking about the nature of learning and influenced our organisation of and interaction with young children.

The views of the Swiss developmental psychologist Jean Piaget had an important effect on educational practice in the 1960s. Prior to this, an attempt had been made to formulate scientific theories of learning, influenced by psychologists such as Ivan Pavlov and B.F. Skinner. According to Wood (1988: 2), Pavlov's work in the 1920s involved teaching animals to make novel 'responses' to new 'stimuli': a dog that naturally salivated for food could be trained to salivate at the sound of a bell before the introduction of food if the bell was rung whenever the food was given. The dog connected the sound of the bell with food. In the 1930s, Skinner, influenced by Pavlov, worked on 'occasional reinforcement' of the desired response and gradual reduction of the reinforcement (ibid.: 3). He applied his ideas on 'shaping behaviour' to teaching. He affirmed that teachers failed because they did not understand the importance of what children already knew and failed to reinforce or build upon it. This work led to teaching schedules based on reinforcement techniques. Evaluation of these frameworks focused on the speed of learning and

15

testing of retention of what had been learned. 'The behaviourist view placed the child in a passive position, and viewed learning simply as a combination of imitation and conditioning by means of external rewards and reinforcements' (Whitebread 1996: 2). The model of learning, suited better for training animals, denied the complexity and flexibility and the potential of the young child.

The work of Piaget became prominent in the 1960s. His most important contribution 'was to alert educators to the child's active role in learning, and the importance of mental activity' (Whitebread 2000: 2). His ideas about learning contrasted with those of Pavlov and Skinner and other so-called behaviourist theorists. Piaget saw the importance of children being active, directing their own learning and being able to solve problems. He offered the idea that human development goes through critical stages, with children not able to learn at the next level until they have passed through the one below. Although his research and writing were not intended to influence education, his theories were widely adopted. They became the framework for a theory of *learning readiness* and were to become a dominant philosophy and to shape a new teaching approach.

Margaret Donaldson (1978) refuted Piaget's view that children were limited in achievement by their developmental stage and lack of logical reasoning. She realised that if children were presented with tasks they did not understand in situations that were unfamiliar to them, they would inevitably fail. If the task was explained to children and the context was familiar to them, then their capacity for learning became extraordinary. Piaget had found that young children were unable to see things from the point of view of others. He had devised tasks with contrived and unfamiliar apparatus. One such experiment used a model of mountains and a small doll. The children were asked to say what the doll could see from a variety of positions. The tendency with this and other experiments was for the children to respond from their own point of view. Donaldson (ibid.) relates the tasks with the same objective devised by Martin Hughes. He had a phenomenal success rate with 90 per cent of a group of 30 three- and four-year-old children clearly able to 'decentre' or to see things from another point of view. He had maintained the purpose of Piaget's experiment but presented his tasks very carefully, using objects such as boys and policemen that made sense to the children. He had also taken time to establish the task and to make sure that the children fully understood what was expected of them.

Jerome Bruner, an American psychologist, worked with Piaget in the 1950s. He shared Piaget's ideas of active learning and problem solving. They both believed that abstract thinking should result from engagement with materials and activities. One of the differences in their thinking was in the ways that language and communication affect learning and the role of the adult in helping children to think and understand.

Lev Vygotsky was a Russian psychologist writing in the 1930s, who had his work translated in the 1960s. Vygotsky influenced Bruner with his ideas on language and communication being at the heart of learning. Bruner saw language as a tool for thinking and conducted experiments that demonstrated that children who were able to use language to describe problems were more likely to succeed than those who lacked the relevant language. Both Vygotsky and Bruner saw the value of children having help from an adult at a point where their own efforts to perform a task fail. This was in contrast to Piaget who believed that children should solve problems unassisted. Vygotsky proposed the *zone of proximal development*. This refers to the gap between what a learner is able to do on his own and what can be achieved with guidance from another person. Bruner developed the idea of 'the spiral curriculum' with children able to take on ideas, regardless of their age, providing that in their early years they understood the task and used practical strategies. As they mature, the same tasks can be revisited and approached from a symbolic or abstract standpoint at a higher and deeper level. These theories have been presented briefly but key issues can still be identified that have influenced the way that we teach young children and use time with them. Table 1.1 identifies some of these issues.

Table 1.1 Learning theories and their effect on educational provision

Learning theories	Influence on early education
Jean Piaget Children being active, directing their own learning and being able to solve problems while interacting with the physical environment	Positive and long lasting influence on provision in many settings with endorsements from contemporary educational policy
Human development goes through critical stages	
This was based on abstract tasks given to children that were set in unfamiliar contexts and introduced by complex language	Led to underestimation of children's capabilities
Children should solve problems unassisted	Led to confusion among practitioners about provision for active learning, and the level of interaction that was appropriate. They were encouraged to be observers and facilitators. Direct teaching was not encouraged
Lev Vygotsky Language and communication is at the heart of learning	Provided a more crucial role for adults in supporting children's learning through appropriate intervention, verbal interaction and extension of children's ideas

'zone of actual development' 'zone of proximal development' 'zone of potential development'	A powerful model that illustrates the way in which a child operates when posed a task – 'actual development', the level that they will achieve with adult support – 'proximal development' and the higher level that is aimed for – 'potential development'
Jerome Bruner 'Language is a tool of thought'	An important tool for adults and children. Appropriate and challenging vocabulary should be introduced as well as encouragement for collaboration and dialogue between peers. The development of language helps children to solve problems and to understand what they are doing.
'The spiral curriculum' Children can learn anything at any age if it is introduced to them in an appropriate way	Adults should be able to provide children with problems set in contexts that they understand. They will then begin to accumulate knowledge that can be used again when they revisit the problem at a higher level
	Children need opportunities to see what is needed in a new situation and to draw on prior knowledge to find a way of proceeding

Educational frameworks that support the effective use of time

A range of philosophical and educational approaches have been chosen for discussion because of the consideration that they give to time and how it may be used in the best interests of children. The approaches which will be discussed are:

- Froebel
- Steiner
- Montessori
- High/Scope
- Te Whariki
- Reggio Emilia.

Froebel

Friedrich Froebel (1782–1852) founded the first kindergarten in 1840. He believed that children learnt outdoors as well as indoors and that children should have time to play in both areas. He also believed in the value of symbolic behaviour and that children needed time to understand and make one thing stand for another. He thought that the best way for children to engage in symbolic behaviour was through their play and that their best thinking occurred when they had time to play. He introduced the idea of free-flow play which, as Bruce (1991: 59) describes, is children 'wallowing in ideas, feelings and relationships'. Wallowing can only occur when considerable time is given for children to experience this way of being.

Steiner

Rudolph Steiner (1861–1925) established his first school in 1919. Time is a constant theme running throughout Steiner education through the curriculum that is offered, the activities which are offered and in the ways adults work with children. Rhythm is important in the curriculum through festivals, seasons, songs and rhymes (Devereux and Miller 2003). It is also apparent in the constant repetition which children experience with a set timetable that has special activities on set days. Many traditional activities undertaken in a Steiner school take time and are approached in a calm, gentle and patient way; activities such as baking, modelling, painting and weaving. Steiner teachers nurture the children in their care and take time to show, explain and teach children. Children also stay with the same teacher for more than one year and this gives teachers time to get to know the children in depth and to fully foster their abilities (de Berker 1999).

Montessori

Dr Maria Montessori (1870–1952) had a different perspective from the previous approaches outlined above. In part, this was due to her training as a doctor and her subsequent work with young children. Unlike Froebel and Steiner, she did not believe in freedom and play but instead emphasised a didactic and controlled approach to working with young, disadvantaged children in Naples. She believed that practitioners needed to take time to show children how to use equipment properly so they might learn. She thought they should take time to talk activities through with children in depth and also for children to have time to be silent and to be absorbed in what they were doing. She also emphasised the need for practitioners to take time to observe children and learn from their observations (Bruce and Meggitt 2002).

High/Scope

This approach originated in a project, directed by David Weikart, for disadvantaged children in Ypsilanti, USA, in the 1960s. It has been subjected to careful evaluation since then and the results of this evaluation have influenced policy-makers, especially the argument for cost-effective nursery education. The key principles underpinning this approach are:

- active learning;
- adult–child interaction;
- learning environment;
- daily routine;
- assessment.

(Hohman and Weikart 1995)

These principles are derived from the work of both Piaget and Vygotsky. Practitioners plan a consistent daily routine for children with time allocated so that children can engage in active learning. Time is allocated so that practitioners can interact with children in a variety of situations: one-to-one, in small groups and as a whole class. Time and the learning environment are organised so that children can follow through their interests and make choices and decisions about where they will work and what they will do. Practitioners also organise their own time to make observations of children and to take part in daily planning sessions in which they share their observations of children. The major feature of the High/Scope approach, which is well known, is the process of *plan–do–review*. This is where time is allocated within the daily routine for children to express their intentions, carry them out and reflect on what they have achieved. This enables children to take control of their learning and become independent learners.

Te Whariki

Te Whariki is the curriculum framework for early childhood education in New Zealand (Ministry of Education 1996). The name means a woven mat and the curriculum framework interweaves central principles, strands and goals. It covers the age range from zero to five years and is divided into three age groups: the infant, the toddler and the young child. The central principles are:

- empowerment – the curriculum empowers the child to learn and grow;
- holistic development – the curriculum reflects the holistic way children learn and grow;
- family and community – the wider world of the child is important;
- relationships – children learn through reciprocal relationships with people, places and things.

There are five strands and these are:

- well-being – the health and well-being of the child are nurtured;
- belonging – children and families have a sense of belonging;

- contribution – each child's contribution is welcomed and valued;
- communication – the languages and symbols of their own and other cultures are promoted;
- exploration – learning takes place through active exploration of the environment.

Throughout the curriculum document time is referred to in the way that children should have time to engage in activities, to communicate with others and for adults to listen and observe: 'adults should take time to listen to views of parents and caregivers' (ibid.: 55).

Reggio Emilia

The Reggio Emilia approach to early education was developed in the northern Italian town of Reggio Emilia in the Reggio Romagno region. It emerged from the persistence of parents, after the Second World War, who recognised that their children had a right to high quality education. By 1963 the first municipal school was opened, based on an approach to education that was living and changing as its protagonists researched different psychological theories, theoretical sources, and evidence from other countries. Their cause was taken up by Loris Malaguzzi who provided continuing inspiration and scholarship. The lasting endurance of the philosophy depends on the collective wisdom of individuals and continual reflection and discourse. The experience for children from birth to six years is based on understanding the following:

- the potential of all children;
- that children do not stand alone but are a part of their family and of the wider community;
- that children have many ways of communication including: drawing, painting, building, shadow play, which became known as 'the hundred languages';
- that the environment is the third teacher – space is designed and used to encourage communication, relationships and use of materials;
- the importance of order and beauty in the organisation of resources and other materials;
- the need for the educators and artists to support children's explorations and problem solving;
- the importance of educators understanding how to observe, plan, listen and respond;
- that documentation is central to the work and depends on careful observation and recording of children's thinking and the thinking of the adults who work with them;

- that documentation will include transcripts, photographs, drawings;
- that parents are partners and will see what is happening through the documentation and be encouraged to contribute ideas, resources and skills;
- that the experience is built on questions. Both children and adults are encouraged to ask questions.

When working with young children we need, at regular intervals, to return to the principles outlined in the curriculum guidance (QCA 2000). Many of these principles require us to rethink the way in which we use time. This chapter has explored some of the many influences on our understanding of early education. In the next chapter, we look at the curriculum and the environment and how they can be organised to allow the time necessary to allow children time to play, to learn and sometimes to stand and stare.

CHAPTER 2

Time to learn

Children's learning is now seen as being limited . . . by their lack of experience and of accumulated knowledge. This makes it more difficult for them to see what is relevant in any new situation, and to see what is the best way to proceed. . . . children's potential for learning is phenomenal and often way beyond our normal expectations.

(Whitebread 2000: 5)

Learning takes time

Those of us who have the privilege of working with young children have a responsibility to ensure that they gain a range of experience and are given time to sort out a learning journey that allows them time to work out what is relevant or irrelevant. Whitebread (ibid.) talks of children's potential for learning as being beyond normal expectations. We will only discover children's potential and review our expectations of them if we understand their development and introduce a flexible approach to time that allows adults and children to stop, look and listen!

The influences of Piaget, Vygotsky and Bruner (see Chapter 1) give us a reason for taking notice of children's developmental stages, allowing them time to explore, to communicate and to work with more experienced adults. In this chapter we are concerned with how time is used to create an interesting, motivating and reflective approach to the curriculum. We look also at how to establish and maintain an environment that is suited to the needs of curious young people.

The vocabulary used in the principles for early years education (QCA 2000: 11) suggests that there should be a sensitive consideration of *time*. Examples of this include, practitioners being able to do the following:

- 'observe and respond appropriately to children';
- 'plan environments and experiences . . . within which children explore, experiment, plan and make decisions for themselves';
- 'provide opportunities for children to plan their own activities and give them time to become engrossed, work in depth and complete activities'.

The principles in the guidance suggest respect for children and their families and the need for time to nurture their development. The curriculum guidance also emphasises that children need time to become secure, with parents and practitioners able 'to discuss each child's circumstances, interests, skills and needs' (ibid.: 9). The importance of home–school links and parental involvement is discussed in Chapter 4.

As practitioners we have to recognise that although the guidance for the Foundation Stage is very valuable, there is a danger that its structure may encourage an over-formality of the curriculum. Children included in the Foundation Stage range in age from 3 to 5 years and we have a responsibility to consider the reality of the curriculum and the environment that we provide for them. We must not fall into the trap of using the six learning areas as a straitjacket. Children need age-appropriate experiences that allow the key objectives for the learning to be achieved holistically. While deciding how we organise the curriculum and the environment there are four important questions to ask:

1 What do we know about the characteristics of young children?
2 Are we giving children time to learn?
3 Are we providing the right conditions for learning?
4 What will help children to exceed our expectations?

The first question is the most important one. Without an understanding of the characteristics of childhood, it is impossible for practitioners to provide a truly effective climate for learning. In Chapter 1 we looked at some of the theories that have helped us to understand how children learn. From these we deduce that children are active learners who learn best in the company of peers and more experienced adults and who need continuous opportunity to communicate and to express their developing ideas. According to Hurst and Joseph (1998), clear vision, practicality, inventiveness, creativity and sensitivity are the qualities that characterise early childhood. Therefore, we must organise time to support this potential not only for learning but also for future citizenship.

The second question relates to time for learning. In order to accommodate dynamic and enthusiastic learners we need to organise the day in a flexible way that allows children to take their time, complete activities, talk about their experiences and receive feedback. Children enjoy a predictable routine but they also flourish when thought has been given to periods where they can concentrate in depth and engage in deep-level learning. Important, also, is the time allowed for listening and for being listened to.

The third question encourages reflection on the quality of provision. The conditions for learning should include meaningful and interesting tasks, challenging situations and intrinsic motivation that comes about when children are 'fascinated by the subject matter and driven to work because of that interest' (Cockburn 2001: 54).

The last question is one that places huge demand on our creative ingenuity, our resourcefulness and our real understanding of the signs that children give us of their potential for hypothesising, breaking boundaries and arriving at unique conclusions. It should cause us to think about:

- our pedagogy or the way that we teach;
- the confidence that we have in interacting with children and observing them;
- our understanding of the power of play and how we accommodate it;
- our ability to assess what children have learned and to see the way forward (this last point is discussed further in Chapter 3).

The curriculum guidance (QCA 2000) provides an important framework for a lively and stimulating curriculum. It is the interpretation of the framework, however, that will either bring the curriculum to life or stultify it. In order to implement the curriculum effectively a creative approach must be employed. In addition, children must have access to an environment that motivates, inspires and enables them to learn to their full potential.

Organising time in practice – the curriculum

Time and the curriculum are inextricably linked especially as according to *The Curriculum Guidance for the Foundation Stage*: 'the term curriculum is used to describe everything children do, see, hear or feel in their setting, both planned and unplanned' (QCA 2000: 1). This then puts a huge onus upon the practitioner to ensure that time is used effectively for children and is not wasted. The curriculum guidance clearly sets out underpinning principles for early years education, one of which refers directly to time: 'children need time to become engrossed, work in depth and complete activities' (ibid.: 11). There then follows guidance for the practitioner on how the principles may be implemented in practice. There is reference to the different ways in which children learn and how practitioners need to draw upon a range of strategies for teaching and caring for children. Over-arching this is the need for a play-based approach to working with young children. This is stated within a separate section on play, within the principles for early years education and is a constant theme running throughout the guidance.

The curriculum framework outlines six separate but inter-related curriculum areas and these are:

- personal, social and emotional development which includes fostering positive dispositions and attitudes to learning, self-esteem and confidence, social relationships, behaviour and self-care;

- communication, language and literacy which includes interacting with others, listening and speaking, language for thinking, reading and writing;
- mathematical development which includes number, shape, space and measures;
- knowledge and understanding of the world which incorporates science, design and technology, history, geography and ICT;
- physical development which includes gross motor skills, fine motor skills and health;
- creative development, which includes art, music, imagination and role-play.

Each area has stepping stones or graduated targets which children must try to achieve during the Foundation Stage. These lead to the final Early Learning Goals to be completed by most children by the end of the reception year.

Analysis of these six areas shows constant reference to the use of time with young children. Some examples from the guidance (QCA 2000) are:

- Personal, social and emotional development – 'ensuring that there is *time* and space for children to focus on activities and experiences and develop their own interests' (p. 28). 'Being with the same adults and children within the setting gives children *time* and opportunity to develop relationships' (p. 29).
- Communication, language and literacy – 'providing *time* and opportunities to develop spoken language through conversations between children and adults, both one-to-one and in small groups' (p. 44).
- Mathematical development – time is an aspect of mathematical development with two distinct strands, one concerned with 'marking specific moments in *time*' and one concerned with 'the passage of *time*' (p. 70).
- Knowledge and understanding of the world – outlined in the section on what the practitioner needs to do for children in this area of learning is the phrase 'give *time* for exploratory play' (p. 87).
- Physical development – 'give sufficient *time* for children to use a range of equipment' (p. 100).
- Creative development – practitioners should give particular attention to 'sufficient *time* for children to explore, develop ideas and finish working at their ideas' (p. 116).

Early years practitioners have generally welcomed the guidance, especially for its emphasis on emergent learning (Siraj-Blatchford and Siraj-Blatchford 2001) and because it provides secure foundations to give children the best possible start in their learning (Staggs 2000). There has, however, been some criticism of the document and its development, stating that it is not based upon children's experiences of learning and is outcome-based, prioritising competitiveness (Soler and

Miller 2003). We would argue, however, that the emphasis on time enshrined in the underpinning principles and throughout the six areas of learning is based upon children's experiences of learning and puts the child at the core of the process of learning and teaching. However, it is no good having a high quality framework if the implementation is not of high quality. This can only occur if practitioners have an understanding of the issues raised in Chapter 1 and reflect upon these in relation to their own practice and modify their practice accordingly. Two further principles also need to be discussed in relation to the early years curriculum. These are a holistic approach to the curriculum and giving children breadth and depth in the curriculum.

An holistic approach to the curriculum

According to Bruce (1997), subjects cannot be separated. Children do not learn mathematics or science or physical education in isolation, because everything is connected. When children are writing, they are not just learning about letter formation and how print works. They are possibly learning mathematics as they attempt to make their letters fit onto the size of paper or other medium they have chosen. They are learning about relationships as they discuss their work with the children around them. They are combining artistic skills as they illustrate their work with pictures and patterns. These skills and understanding are interlinked and help to provide children with a wider view of how the world works. Therefore, not only does there need to be a consideration of time for children to engage in aspects of the curriculum, there also needs to be a consideration of time for children to engage in a holistic approach to their learning.

Breadth and depth in the curriculum

Bruce states that the curriculum should 'engage children both broadly and deeply with the content of the curriculum' (1997: 63). Therefore, in order for children to learn effectively, children need time to learn widely about subjects that interest them and to relate different areas of learning to their underlying interest. They need to learn a range of skills, knowledge, understanding and attitudes concerned with their subject of interest. However, they also need time to learn in depth about a subject, to learn about detail connected with their area of interest. In addition, practitioners need to give themselves time to enable them to take children's learning to a deeper level.

A child with, for example, an interest in dinosaurs needs to explore aspects of this interest widely through making scenarios for dinosaurs out of clay and natural materials, reading fiction and non-fiction books about dinosaurs, painting and drawing dinosaurs and moving like a dinosaur during physical activities. The child will also need to explore dinosaurs in depth, differentiating dinosaurs according to their diet, finding out the names and habitats of different dinosaurs,

going on a museum trip to look at dinosaur bones and fossils. In engag-
se activities, the child will gain new understanding, knowledge, skills and
Finally, the practitioner will have to take time to further their own
knowledge about dinosaurs in order to take the child's learning further.

Planning the curriculum over time

The curriculum needs to be carefully planned over time to ensure that all areas of
learning are addressed and children have opportunities to achieve the stepping
stones and early learning goals. The timetable also needs to be carefully planned
to ensure that children receive a holistic curriculum and one that provides them
with depth and breadth. The curriculum needs to be planned over the course of an
academic year – long-term planning, over a half term – medium-term planning,
and over a week – short-term planning. Some examples of these types of planning
are given in the guidance for early years entitled *Planning for Learning in the Foundation Stage* (QCA 2001). The examples of planning presented in this chapter have
been chosen because of the integrity of the authors, the collaboration between
practitioners and the evidence of understanding of the needs of young children.
Any grid format for planning inhibits the planner. Plans of this nature need
constant review so that time can be used appropriately for individual children and
groups of children.

Long-term planning

Fisher (2002a) states that the aim of long-term planning is to ensure that children
receive a broad and balanced curriculum. It can be argued, however, that children
are entitled to a broad and balanced curriculum all the time and that this should
be evident at all stages of planning. The primary purpose of long-term planning is
concerned with children's entitlement to the curriculum. Long-term plans should
show that sensitive and careful thought has been given to how children will build
up their knowledge, understanding, skills and attitudes across all curriculum areas
over the year. Table 2.1 shows how one nursery school has carefully thought
through how children may progress in personal, social and emotional development over the school year. Consideration has been given to children attending
part-time and full-time and all aspects of the nursery session have been accounted
for, including tidy-up time. The development across each term is signalled using
different font – normal font for the autumn term, bold font for the spring term
and italics for the summer term.

Table 2.1 Progression in personal, social and emotional development

	Personal, social and emotional experience	ELGs
Autumn term	Re-establish & build positive relationships with staff and peers – including Full Time induction.	2,7
	Learn to manage a new situation, without the constant presence of parent/carer/significant adult.	5,7,8,14
	Take care of their own needs (toilet, coats, aprons).	5,11
	Begin to understand & participate in daily routine (Full & Part Time) – observation>active participation – maximise opportunities.	4
	Have an awareness of being part of a small group, class/es, lunchtime and whole school group.	3,6,8,10,13, K10
	Begin to make appropriate choices and decisions – planning, behaviour and play – returners to model.	1,3,8,9,10,12
	Begin to understand the need to care, share and tidy – returners to model.	12
Spring term	**Begin the New Year with confidence, showing increased involvement levels & interest in their work.**	1,2
	Take care of their own needs (toilet, coats, aprons) – **growing in independence.**	5,11
	Participate in daily routine and **manage change within it e.g. visit to the gym.**	2,4
	Show awareness, **tolerance & understanding of other's feelings & needs – including new children.**	4–8,13,K11
	Make appropriate choices and decisions – planning, **environment**, behaviour, play **& for some children to share their ideas.**	3,7–10,12,13
	Make progress in contributing to the caring and tidying **of equipment and environment.**	12
Summer term	*Become independent* **in managing** *self help skills and help one another.*	5,11
	Show increased involvement levels and interest in their work – *and encourage independence in one another.*	1,2
	Manage change *in new situation with confidence* (Gym, Transition), *demonstrating real ownership of the daily routine.*	2,4,13,14
	Show tolerance & understanding of other's feelings & needs – to negotiate and share *across the groups.*	5–8,10,13,14
	Make appropriate & *considered* choices and decisions – planning, **environment**, behaviour, play **& for** *most* **children to share their ideas.**	1,2,8,9,12,L6
	Make a contribution to & *understand that everyone is* **responsible for the** caring and tidying of **equipment.**	8

Medium-term planning

Fisher (2002a) states that she feels that this is the most problematic of all areas of planning. Children's development involves rapid change and it is impossible to plan accurately, therefore, much medium-term planning is focused around a central theme or themes. Ideally these themes or theme should derive from the children's own interests and ideas following the Reggio Emilia approach to early years education (introduced in Chapter 1) but this practice is not usual within many of our schools. Usually predetermined learning intentions drive the planning and then week-by-week different activities provide the vehicle for children to achieve the learning intentions. Theme-based planning provides the opportunity to make cross-curricular links and can ensure a holistic curriculum, and breadth and depth, but this is as likely from a child-initiated theme as from an adult-initiated one. When planning from children's ideas, the content becomes more meaningful to the child and opportunities for sustained shared thinking and in-depth work become more likely.

A different way of planning for the medium term is from the children's interests in different activity areas. This way of planning is much more responsive to the needs of children and is completed across a shorter time-span, three to four weeks instead of a half-term. The learning is clearly holistic as each area of the class caters for different activities and different areas of learning. Breadth and depth are also achieved by staff actively respecting and considering these aspects of the curriculum when making their plans. Table 2.2 is an example of this type of planning and is taken from the same nursery school as the example of long-term planning. The medium-term planning needs to be read in conjunction with the long-term planning as this is where the learning goals are explicitly indicated. The first column shows adult observation of the area of the class, the second column shows how the plan builds on the observation. Planning is shown for two areas of the classroom. Considerable discussion and team working are required to make this type of planning successful. There is also shared understanding of the issues raised in Chapter 1 and how this impacts on their practice and implementation of the curriculum.

Table 2.2 Medium-term planning from activity areas

Observation of areas	Plans – Focus/workshops and Learning intentions	ELGs
Weeks ending 31st Jan		
Art		
Introduction of Christmassy resources brought all children into area. Some went into 'mass production'. Some have continued in the area and are making	Build on this interest – exciting resources – introduce connections net for hanging smaller pieces of work. Connection resources placed in	C1 P4

decision and selecting resources independently. Lots of paint based activities – some need some highlighting of self organisation/ technique. Regular use of sand and water used in variety of ways – developing interests e.g. imaginative-exploratory-scientific-maths	boxes – pipe cleaners, bulldog clips, clothes pegs, paper clips. These will be in addition to staples, sellotape, treasury tags etc already there. Highlight techniques and support organisation of resources e.g. routine of selecting what you need, carrying out work and then clearing up. Raise awareness of blocks paints inside (already good use outside)	M5 K4 PS6

Quiet

Continue to include stories and mark making in play. Book Share has been highlighted again – stories read from new box and lots of children have borrowed books. Puzzles not used regularly and difficult to support – not completed.	Have we a parent who would read first thing – worked well last year! Ensure two differentiated stories a week in group time at end of session. Introduce new shape games/puzzles. Continue to value/support work with puzzles. Revamp sewing trolley	L3 L2 K5,6 M3

Weeks ending 12th March

Art

Connections displayed as hanging models. Techniques highlighted – connections tray children using resources. Children revisiting by looking up at models – recognising their own. Lots of printing based activities – tactile experiences – painting hands, arms etc. Resources limited in water tray – has helped for selection. Role play often involved – making cakes etc. Sand in regular use – changed resources to highlight different small cups etc.	Highlighting 3D model making resources – put container of boxes on small table – ready for selection. Arrange and rearrange resources. Adult's present/motivate opportunities for exploring different combinations/connecting etc. Raise awareness of printing resources – different shapes and textures e.g. sponges, corks, bricks etc. Time to wallow – to use resources appropriately – modelled by adults.	P4 C1 K4

Quiet

More stories read in worktime – 1-to-1 and small groups. Still often difficult to have a story at end of session am & pm new children need to settle. Regular use of games and puzzles – lots of group play with and without adult. Some interest in sewing in am & pm – developing needle skills.	Continue to read stories in worktime, introduce more group stories. J use page-turner to read books independently. Highlight Book share in storytime and encourage use. Introduce two new puzzles – go alongside some new IT work – fitting things together. Add animals/zoo resources	L3 M5

Short-term planning

Short-term planning provides evidence of the intended weekly programme. Activities are planned for in depth and can be much more responsive to children's needs and development. Short-term plans should include the range of learning offered by the curriculum as well as how time will be spent outside and inside. Table 2.3 is an example of a weekly plan from a reception class in an infant school. Learning intentions are indicated along with activities for indoors and outdoors. A system is in place in the class to observe children's responses to the activities and their ideas are then fed into the planning on a daily basis and so the short-term plan becomes an ever changing document.

Table 2.3 Weekly plan from a reception class

Foundation Stage Planning
Weekly planning

Personal, Social and Emotional Development

Learning Intention: * To consider the consequences of their own actions. * To recognise how we can stay safe on the road. * To consider others.

Indoor Activities	Outdoor Activities
Resources: 'Look out on the road', small world road map, cars, playpeople, road signs.	Resources: Wheeled toys, road safety equipment, train set, playpeople, cars, road signs.
Activities: ● Circle time – identifying how we can stay safe on the road and near transport. ● Using small world equipment to create road and train maps with zebra crossings, traffic lights, level crossings etc.	Activities: ● Using wheeled toys to consider how we can stay safe when travelling on and crossing the road. ● Using small world equipment to create road and train maps with zebra crossings, traffic lights, level crossings etc

Communication, Language and Literacy

Learning Intention: * To use features of postcards in their own writing. * To use talk to organise, sequence & clarify thinking, ideas, feelings & events. * To read and write the letters that represent 'ch'. * To hear and write initial, final and short vowel sounds with CVC words.

Indoor Activities	Outdoor Activities
Resources: card, postcards, sorting objects, writing implements.	Resources: Role-play equipment, chalk, brushes, paint, laminated key words.
Activities: ● Writing postcards to our friends in class. ● Playing pass the parcel, jump in the	Activities: ● Role-play area – service station: sending and writing postcards.

hoop, NSEW etc. to identify initial, final and short vowel sounds within CVC words.
- Forming the letters 'ch' using pencils, pens, paint etc.
- Describing models, plans, adaptations and materials.

- Forming the letters 'ch' using chalks, water and paint.
- Searching for key words in the trees.

Mathematical Development

Learning Intention: * To compare and estimate up to three capacities. * To use developing mathematical ideas to solve practical problems. * To count to 100 in 10's.

Indoor Activities
Resources: Suitcases of different sizes, role-play equipment, containers & objects.

Outdoor Activities
Resources: Containers of different sizes, chalk & dice, laminated numerals to 100.

Activities:
- Packing suitcases, bags and picnic baskets for a journey.
- Using construction materials to build vehicles for a certain number of people, objects etc.
- Counting on and back to 100 in 10's.

Activities:
- Filling containers of various sizes in the water tray.
- Going on a number journey using chalked numbers on the floor.
- Searching for numerals in the trees.

Time and the Literacy and Numeracy Strategies

The influence of the National Literacy and Numeracy Strategies (NLS and NNS) on the use of time in reception classes has been an ongoing issue since their introduction in 1998 and 1999 respectively. Both Strategies were introduced in an attempt to raise educational standards in primary schools and they provide a framework for teaching literacy and numeracy from reception to year 6. From the beginning early years practitioners were concerned about the impact of the Strategies on early years education but there was particular concern regarding the NLS with its emphasis on teaching through a 'literacy hour' (Whitehead 1999; Fisher 2000). However, the NLS document explicitly states that the full Literacy Hour does not need to be introduced until the end of the reception year and this is further exemplified in the guidance document for the organisation of the NLS in reception classes (DfEE 2000). Despite this guidance, Ofsted (2000) reported that most teachers do implement the Literacy Hour by the end of the autumn term.

Many would argue that the implementation of such a formal experience for young children can be inhibiting. Cousins, writing in 1999, said that it was the only time during her research with four-year-olds that she saw them get agitated. Klein (2000) asserted that sitting still for such long periods of time was damaging for posture and health. McInnes (2001) found that the effect of focusing so much time on a full Literacy Hour led to a decrease in the breadth of the curriculum offered to the children. In addition, children did not engage in in-depth activities

Table 2.4 Reception class timetable

	9.00 – 9.20	9.20 – 10.30	10.30 – 11.00	11.00 – 11.50	11.50 – 12.00	12.00 – 1.15	1.15 – 1.30	1.30 – 2.45	2.45 – 3.10
M	Registration Celebration Circle time Communication, Language and Literacy	Small group time Communication, Language and Literacy Mathematical Development Independent planning – inside/outside Six areas of development	Plenary Milk and Fruit Class assembly	Small group time Communication, Language and Literacy Mathematical Development Independent planning – inside/outside Six areas of development	Plenary	Lunch time	Registration Circle time Mathematical Development	Small group time Communication, Language and Literacy Mathematical Development Independent planning – inside/outside Six areas of development	Plenary Story
T	Registration Celebration Circle time Communication, Language and Literacy	Small group time Communication, Language and Literacy Mathematical Development Independent planning – inside/outside Six areas of development	Plenary Milk and Fruit Mathematical Development	Small group time Communication, Language and Literacy Mathematical Development Independent planning – inside/outside Six areas of development	Plenary	Lunch time	Registration Circle time Personal, Social and Emotional Development	Small group time Communication, Language and Literacy Mathematical Development Independent planning – inside/outside Six areas of development	Plenary Story
W	Registration Celebration Circle time Creative Development	Small group time Creative Development Communication, Language and Literacy Independent planning – inside/outside Six areas of development	Plenary Milk and Fruit Mathematical Development	Hall time Physical Development Creative Development		Lunch time	Registration Circle time Knowledge and Understanding of the World	Small group time Knowledge and Understanding of the World Communication, Language and Literacy Independent planning – inside/outside Six areas of development	Plenary Story
T	Registration Celebration Circle time Mathematical Development	Small group time Creative Development Mathematical Development Independent planning – inside/outside Six areas of development	Plenary Milk and Fruit	Hall time Physical Development		Lunch time	Registration Library skills Communication, Language and Literacy	Small group time Creative Development Communication, Language and Literacy Independent planning – inside/outside Six areas of development	Plenary Story
F	Registration Celebration Circle time Mathematical Development	Small group time Knowledge and Understanding of the World Mathematical Development Independent planning – inside/outside Six areas of development	Plenary Milk and Fruit	Small group time Knowledge and Understanding of the World Mathematical Development Independent planning – inside/outside Six areas of development	Plenary	Lunch time	Registration Circle time Communication, Language and Literacy	Small group time Knowledge and Understanding of the World Communication, Language and Literacy Independent planning – inside/outside Six areas of development	Plenary Story

nor were there opportunities for sustained shared thinking in the class where the full hour was in place.

So can a balance be achieved between fulfilling the requirements of the Strategies and ensuring that children do not spend too much of their time sitting on their bottoms? Table 2.4 shows a timetable from a reception class where children cover all elements of the Literacy and Numeracy Strategies but in a way that is appropriate to their age and stage of development. Each day is broken down into smaller periods of time, which consist of whole class times, small group times and independent planning times. Each element of the day is clearly marked to indicate which area of the curriculum they are focusing on. In addition, times such as registration and milk and fruit time are also used to work on elements such as counting. Children in this class cover all the elements of the Literacy and Numeracy Strategies, have opportunities to engage in activities in depth and are able to learn in a way that fulfils all the elements for learning outlined in Chapter 1 (Dowling 1992; Fisher 2002a).

Organising time – the learning environment

> An environment is a living, changing system. More than physical space, it includes the way it is structured and the roles we are expected to play. It conditions how we feel, think and behave; and it dramatically affects the quality of our lives. The environment either works for us or against us as we conduct our lives.
>
> (Greenman 1988: 5, cited in Edwards *et al.* 1998: 169)

Are we aware of the importance of the environment in which we live and of the importance of the environment that we share with young children? The fast pace of daily life is all too often mirrored in an inappropriate pace of life in many early years settings. In the hurry to achieve targets, how often do we stop to reflect on the quality of the surroundings or identify anomalies and inconsistencies in the use of time? The schedule reproduced in Table 2.5 came from a student teacher. The children were in a reception class and the student had used this schedule in her dissertation in which she was debating the rhetoric and reality of a play-based curriculum.

The timetable shows restricted division of children's time and a worrying lack of active experience. (The emboldened type represents blocks of time spent on sedentary experience and the normal type the active experience.) These children spent just over 6 hours in school and nearly 5 hours doing sedentary, predetermined activities. This is surely not acceptable? From the timetable we can make inferences about the quality of the classroom provision.

- The children spent much of the day sitting down on chairs at tables, on 'the carpet' or on the floor.
- The 'free play' time was short with no evidence of planning for play. We can

Table 2.5 A daily timetable in one reception class

Time	Activity	Minutes
8.50	Enter classroom, settle on the carpet for register and explanation of maths activity 'roamers'. Whole-class teaching	**40 min**
9.30	In groups embark on the 'roamer' activity	20 min
9.50	Gather on carpet for discussion of activity and learning outcomes	**25 min**
10.15	Whole school assembly – theme 'dislikes'	**25 min**
10.40	Break time – children outside	20 min
11.00	Drinks and music on the carpet, then circle time when children talk about what they are looking forward to. Explanation of next activity	**20 min**
11.20	Literacy group work – theme 'I love'	**30 min**
11.50	Carpet time where some children show their finished work to the group	**25 min**
12.15	Lunch	**20 min**
12.35	Play outside	25 min
1.00	Carpet time where the remainder of the children show their work to the rest of the class	**15 min**
1.15	Groups alternate to make fruit salad sitting at tables. The remainder of the class finish off their literacy or numeracy work	**65 min**
2.20	Whole class has free play option	20 min
2.40	Carpet time for 'show and tell'	**20 min**
3.00	Children get ready to go home – collect belongings, letters, etc.	15 min
3.15	Children go home	

infer that resources are limited or that there was a lack of understanding of how to enable self-initiated planning for play.

- The curriculum appears to be restricted and the environment possibly impoverished.
- Time had been apportioned to activities with no regard for their suitability or for the need for children to be active and interactive.

Can assumptions be made on the evidence of a timetable for one day? In this book we try to be fair. We present positive scenarios, as is evident earlier in the chapter. It is easy to criticise the practice of other professionals! It is less easy to reflect on one's own practice and less easy still to make changes. Two questions to address are: What are the characteristics of environments that support the all-round development of young children, and what are some of the strategies for organising and developing effective learning environments?

When we plant seeds, take cuttings or compost vegetable matter, we are eager to do research. As recent converts to gardening, we are happy to read, discuss with more experienced gardeners and generally take advice on how things should be done. However, there seems to be a reluctance to take advice on how to achieve the best climate and conditions for children's learning. The curriculum and the environment should be inextricably linked. Practitioners, however, often set up environments that reflect their own taste and personal view of children. In these cases there is no philosophical or pedagogical underpinning and no link between the strong principles outlined in the guidance and the reality of the provision. This was clearly illustrated in Table 2.2.

The Curriculum Guidance for the Foundation Stage (QCA 2000: 14) requires practitioners to do the following:

- 'plan a learning environment indoors and outdoors, that encourages a positive attitude to learning';
- provide an environment where 'time is allowed for sustained concentration' (ibid.: 15);
- provide an environment 'where sessions include adult- and child-planned activities, with uninterrupted time for children to work in depth' (ibid.: 16).

If we accept that *the curriculum* for young children 'describes everything children do, see, hear or feel in their setting, both planned and unplanned' (ibid.: 1) then we need to adopt a similarly broad understanding of the *environment*. The term *environment* refers to physical learning spaces and to the adults and children who spend time in it. It further refers to support for learning that includes respect, motivation, values, ideas and resources. Williams (2003: 74–82) provides a useful framework to help practitioners reflect on characteristics that shape positive learning environments. The framework recommends a close look at the following features.

The physical space

How the space is organised will determine how adults and children can interact. The space is defined and will have inherent constraints but the organisation should allow children time to be independent, responsible and empathetic with others.

What is in the space will provide a window on the curriculum or, as Moyles (1995) talks about, a bird's eye view of the classroom providing a map of the curriculum that is possibly in place and a good idea of the teaching and learning style. What furniture has been chosen, how much of it there is and how it is organised will determine the amount of movement that is possible and the opportunities for children to be creative, and active. Often there are areas that are under-used, possibly because no time has been taken to review the physical organisation of the learning space.

Figure 2.1 illustrates large- and small-scale experiences of children. In both cases the children have the opportunity to use materials freely and at their own pace. The photographs give us a clear insight into the curriculum values and the teaching and learning styles held by the staff in the settings.

Figure 2.1 Children using materials freely and being given time to work at their own pace

Resources

'Resources are intended to support learning and give children the chance to inter-act with a range of commercial and improvised artefacts' (Williams 2003: 79). Important considerations are the relevance of resources for all the children, their organisation and the opportunities that they afford for a holistic approach to learning. Young children need to be excited by artefacts. Artefacts, both impro-vised and commercial, should encourage children to spend time in 'continuing curiosity, exploration, investigation and discovery' (Fisher 1996: 66). Think about the resources that you use with children and consider how they have been chosen, how you decide on additional ones, what scope they have for developing cognitive understanding and whether they have any relevance for the children in your group. Take time to talk to children about the popular culture that is a part of their lives outside school and probably their lives in the playground. What elements of this popular culture would be of benefit in the classroom?

Displays

Displays can be a serious bone of contention. Williams (2003: 78) says: 'Many schools (settings) have an "in house style" that may involve hours of preparation, with prestige gained by those who achieve the ideal.' Displays will also reflect the personal aesthetic style of the practitioner that may be at odds with the people who have to look at the display. Why are we so obsessed by displays? Displays, of whatever nature, reflect personal taste. They do not necessarily reflect the diverse cultural experience of children nor do they provide a 'sensitive, interactive and in-formative advertisement for the whole curriculum' (ibid.: 79). Can the time spent on mounting a display be really justified? There is a further discussion of spaces, resources and displays when the Reggio Emilia approach to early education is dis-cussed later in the chapter.

In the previous section of this chapter there was a useful analysis of the six areas of learning (QCA 2000) and the relationship that they have with time. Reflecting on time in this context helps to determine the characteristics of a supportive environment. The environment should provide opportunities for:

- relationships to develop and children to develop a sense of well-being;
- focusing on activities and developing interests;
- developing spoken language;
- understanding 'moments in time' and 'the passage of time';
- being involved in exploratory play;
- using a range of equipment to help physical development;
- children to develop creativity by exploring, developing ideas and staying with their work in order to finish it.

Williams (2003) reflects on the environment and the support that it can give to children's independence. She suggests an audit of provision in the classroom and ways to review and improve it. This technique has been adapted to consider not only independence but also the use of time. Questions might well include:

1 Which aspects of daily organisation need modification in order to allow children more time to think and to respond independently?

2 Learning in the early years is an holistic experience. How can subject-oriented bays (maths, writing, science) be justified?

3 How does the physical environment reflect the needs of active, enquiring children who need time to absorb and process information and build on their existing knowledge of the world?

4 Is the 'carpet' a refuge for children to sometimes read quietly, discuss with peers, spend time in quiet reflection or is it always used as the position for didactic teacher-led exposition?

5 Are children encouraged to talk about their lives outside the school and to contribute their knowledge and ideas to the curriculum?

6 Where are the opportunities for children to spend time in active learning?

7 How much time is given to observing children and modifying the planned curriculum to develop more appropriate experiences?

8 What resources are on offer, what time do children have to use them, how do they support children's all-round learning?

This is a revealing audit. It may cause despair and defence! It is, however, important that we reflect on provision and do not allow perceived constraints to spoil what should be an exciting time in the lives of small children.

Environments that are caring spaces

In the past five years there has been a growing interest in the work of the municipal pre-schools, for three- to five-year-olds, in the northern Italian town of Reggio Emilia. Visiting these schools brings about a sense of awe and wonder! The characteristics of the environments are very visible. How they have been achieved makes interesting reading (for detailed information about the history and management of the Reggio Emilia approach, see Edwards *et al.* 1998).

The Reggio Emilia approach is developing out of a carefully thought-out philosophy and an educational programme that results from discussion, experimentation, reflection and change. The structure of the learning space, its arrangement and management are designed to complement the programme. The characteristics include transparency where possible, with maximum light and continuity between inside and outside. The centres are placed in view of the public and have become an integral part of the neighbourhood.

When visiting the schools in Reggio Emilia the first impression of the environment is the space, the light and the lack of clutter. There is a sense of well-being for children and adults. The space gives a clear message about the care and the educational opportunities afforded to the children. There is workshop space, including the ateliers or art workshops, where children can work in groups and private spaces in which children can be alone. The central *piazza* is used for meetings, discussions and exchange of ideas. Space in the neighbourhood environment is valued. Using this space is a regular part of the extensive project work. The environments work well. When reading about an educational system or visiting settings, it is important to realise that the process cannot be simply transported into our own settings. We should, however, be prepared to put aside any preconceived ideas and deliberate on what is making the environment work and what strategies we can use to improve our own provision. As well as space, light and lack of clutter, there is an invitation to explore. Large structures created by children and adults, simple, beautifully designed furniture and plentiful improvised and natural materials invite exploration. Any commercial items have been carefully chosen and are replicated in all the schools. These include the fascinating glass-lined prism, projection equipment and the well-used light tables. The layout of the space and the organisation of the resources encourage communication, exchange of ideas and interaction.

The curriculum in the Reggio preschools is determined through project work. Children's ideas are picked up by teachers, shared with colleagues and supported with discussion, materials and tools. The use of the space is a determinant of the success of the projects. The organisation of the staff means that each adult has equal value and has time to give children a high level of attention when necessary.

Time is given to children to work at their own pace and because there is a policy for children to remain with the same teachers for three years (from three years to six years), there is time to develop thoroughly without the pressure of continual changes. There is constant reflection about the daily happenings and careful documentation of individual and group experience that can be displayed and shared with parents and visitors. Walls are not used to create displays in the way that we understand them.

How space is used reflects the culture of the people who have created it. The use of space in Reggio schools reflects the culture of northern Italy. Essential cultural elements include:

- beauty, harmony and design;
- an environment that favours social interaction;
- regional food prepared freshly;
- involvement (through project work) with the neighbourhood.

What is the relevance of this discussion to children's time spent in our own early years settings? 'Spaces could look more or less alike but if they are a part of a culture and subject to some pedagogical reflection about their use, their significance changes completely' (Gandini, in Edwards *et al.* 1998: 165).

Many traditional settings have large spaces, similar to the *piazza* in the Reggio schools. The difference is in the way in which these valuable spaces are used. The important consideration is that there should be a philosophical basis from which to operate that helps to identify the really effective use of time and space. With the Reggio approach and its strong philosophy and pedagogical influence, there are common elements in all the schools. These include attention to detail, care of the spaces, creative and flexible use of artefacts and furniture, a sympathetic understanding of the use of time for adults and children, and reflection on the lives of the particular group of children. In spite of these commonalities, each school is individual. In Chapter 3 there is further discussion of the approach. The lasting impression of the Reggio schools is one of serenity and beauty and a feeling that there is always time for adults and for children.

Time to assess

> In assessing learning, the act of seeing gives way to the act of understanding; the process of collecting evidence is followed by attempts to make the evidence meaningful.
>
> (Drummond 1994: 70)

Assessment

In the previous chapters we have considered how children learn and how time for the curriculum and the environment can be organised to maximise learning. In this chapter we are concerned with assessment and the range of assessment strategies that help us decide what children are learning and what the next stage of the learning journey should be. One of the shortcomings of the post-Plowden Report era (CACE 1966) was the failure of practitioners to keep records of children's achievement. Looking back on some of the excellent early years practice at that time it seems that practitioners were, unfortunately, very protective of their knowledge of young children's development. When challenged, they failed to justify the reasons for the success of their stimulating and challenging environments and creative curriculums. Maybe their training did not equip them to reflect on practice or to articulate their principles. Maybe there was scepticism on behalf of trainers as to the move towards a more holistic approach to learning.

We are now required, quite rightly, to record and assess and use assessments to help with forward planning, provide information on children's all-round development and diagnosis of possible problems. Assessment should be seen as an integral part of the teaching and learning continuum. Evidence from assessment should be shared between professional colleagues, as well as at an intimate, teacher/child/parent level and at local level and even at national level.

Informal assessment

Experienced adults will be assessing informally from their first encounter with children. Ideally this will start when they visit a child's home (see Chapter 4) or a child's previous setting. Practitioners will watch, listen and allow time for real conversation. Informal assessment requires practitioners to use their understanding of child development to make sense of what they have observed. Evidence from observations should be used to support curriculum planning and planning the environment. A new group of children will bring with them a variety of prior experiences, skills and knowledge. Care has to be taken to welcome them and be acutely aware of their developing understanding.

Experienced early years practitioners are successful, informal assessors who are then able to use their time to make sensible use of the evidence. Evidence gathered from informal assessment should have an immediate impact on the curriculum and any adaptations that need to be made to the forward planning. We have to be realistic. Practitioners will not achieve the aims of informal assessment unless time is organised to allow for the strategies discussed later and priority is given to 'stopping, looking and listening'. How many of us really consider that standing back and observing children is as important as directing them or interacting with them? If we do understand that evidence of children's understanding can be observed and recorded in a variety of ways, how much time do we give to these activities? Do we also allow time to interpret the observations and use it to really inform the way forward?

In the Reggio Emilia approach to early education (see Edwards *et al.* 1998), there is powerful use of *documentation*. Photographs, children's questions and responses, evidence of their development in thinking or their different responses to a problem are used not just as a display but as a visible means of evaluating the effectiveness of the teaching and learning of some of the children. Documentation is an ongoing informal assessment process that allows adults to study the thought patterns and actions of children. Using, sustaining and developing documentation are discussed in the last section of this chapter.

Formal assessment

The use of formal assessment raises questions of reliability and validity. As Haylock (in Cockburn 2001: 118) says, we must ask the questions: 'Can we rely on the results of the assessment?' and 'Does the assessment actually assess what it purports to assess?' Further points to consider when using formal assessment with very young children are whether the assessments are really necessary, whether formal assessment is taking time away from continuity of children's experience, and what use will be made of the evidence from the assessment. Formal assessment may take the form of tests or, often with younger children, check lists. The *Foundation Stage Profile* (QCA 2003) is an example of this. The mistaken belief is that filling out a checklist is an expedient way of assessing children. The danger with the use of checklists is that practitioners do not take time to learn about individual children and tend to organise the curriculum around the required check list outcomes. If assessment is restricted in this way, the curriculum may become narrow and fashioned only to satisfy the assessment requirements.

Why should we assess young children?

'[E]ffective assessment is a process in which our understanding of children's learning, acquired through observation and reflection, can be used to evaluate and enrich the curriculum we offer' (Drummond 1994: 13). Assessment certainly helps us to decide what children are learning and what the next stage of the learning journey should be. This is particularly important for medium- and long-term planning as discussed in Chapter 2. Assessment is equally important for:

- diagnosis: awareness of individual children's strengths or weaknesses including observation of children's likes, dislikes and schematic patterns of behaviour;
- encouragement and motivation: raising children's esteem and stimulating their enthusiasm when assessment of individual and group progress is shared with them;
- making teaching and learning visible to colleagues and parents: providing evidence of children's social, academic, physical, and creative progress;
- providing genuine developmental information to satisfy statutory requirements for assessment which means at this time completing the Foundation Stage Profile (QCA 2003).

The downside of any assessment technique is the time it takes and many practitioners feel that it is not time well spent. Their argument is that writing up lengthy observations takes time away from the children. Carr (2001: 94) suggests that 'a balance needs to be struck where the time and effort required by more elaborated processes is manageable and practicable and the assessments are interesting and enjoyable'.

How we use time to assess

Now that the argument for assessment has been made and the necessity for practitioners to make time to assess been discussed, we now focus on how we use time to assess. Who does the assessment? Is this the preserve of teachers or are all adults who work with and interact with young children responsible for the assessment of their development and learning? What gets assessed? The obvious answer is that children get assessed but what aspects of their development and learning need to be assessed and do we need to consider anything else? When does assessment take place? Many would argue that assessment occurs all the time, but does it really and is this effective use of our valuable time? Finally, we need to address the 'how' of assessment. There are many models, techniques and schedules of assessment, which practitioners can use to assess young children, however, which ones are the most time-efficient in that they provide valuable and usable information but are not time-onerous to complete?

Who does the assessment?

In the introduction to this section on how we use time to assess, the question was raised as to whether assessment is the preserve of teachers. We would argue that all adults who interact and work with young children are responsible for contributing to assessment and this includes parents. When children begin the Foundation Stage, the people who know them best are their parents and carers and they need to have input into their initial assessment. This is often carried out through the completion of 'welcome to school books' and 'all about me documents', where parents state their children's likes, dislikes, interests and strengths. However, parents and carers should contribute in an ongoing and two-way process through constant dialogue with practitioners and sharing children's interests, strengths and other pertinent information.

Adults who interact with the children in different contexts should play a part in the assessment process and contribute to ongoing records. It may be that a child is with a childminder in the morning and nursery in the afternoon and therefore there should be dialogue between the childminder and the nursery, with both parties contributing to each other's records. A child may be receiving input from other professionals, for example, attending speech and language therapy and therefore the views of the other professionals should be sought and documented. How this is to be done provides an opportunity for dialogue and co-operation.

During the child's time in the Foundation Stage there will be many different adults who will potentially work with the child, from a variety of early years practitioners to helpers and students. All these people need to contribute to the assessment process and systems need to be in place to guide them in making relevant and purposeful contributions. Finally, it must be remembered that the child also has a part to play in assessment and there needs to be opportunity for them to voice their views and opinions, for these to be taken seriously and to be acted upon.

Who does the assessment is a complex issue and many practitioners will be wary of asking non-professionals to contribute and certainly wary about including children, but if we believe that we need to obtain a full and true picture of the child's learning and development, then it is important to collect a range of views. It also will take time to put systems in place to ensure that all can contribute effectively as Lally and Hurst (in Blenkin and Kelly 1992: 73) state: 'involving a range of people in assessment sounds much more straightforward than it actually is. Involvement takes time and there is never enough. It also requires people to trust one another, and to listen to one another's views.' However, ultimately it will be time well spent and time used effectively for adults and children.

What is assessed?

According to Pascal and Bertram (in Fisher 2002b: 92), 'We need to ensure that what we are measuring truly matters and that we are not simply focusing on those things that are easily measured.' Obviously children need to be assessed, but what particular aspects of children's development and learning need to be assessed? There needs to be a focus on children's attitudes to learning as these underpin all other aspects and are the key to learning. Key questions need to be asked concerning independence, creativity and motivation. The ability of children to socialise with others and form relationships needs to be assessed as does their emotional well-being. Their interests need to be identified. What individual children enjoy doing and what they are drawn to and how they prefer to spend their time are questions needing answers. The answers will provide a way forward to make children feel secure. Children need to show what they can do and this should provide the basis for curriculum planning and development based on their interests.

Children's knowledge and skills also need to be assessed, through identifying what children can do across all areas of the curriculum and during child-initiated activities as well as adult-initiated activities. This will then enable practitioners to comment on children's overall development, to note strengths, areas for concern and to share this information with other people. To be able to do this effectively, time will need to be spent on ensuring that a curriculum is planned which ensures breadth and depth and to which practitioners have an holistic approach, as described in Chapter 2.

However, it is not only children that need to be assessed. Time also needs to be taken to assess the provision that is on offer to young children. There are questions that should form a framework for assessing the provision in the setting.

1 Which areas of the setting are used frequently by children?

2 Which areas are under-used?

3 Which resources are used?

4 How well are the resources used?

5 Should adults be assessed?

This final question is one that often raises fear in the minds of practitioners; however, if we are to improve our practice and continually strive to be reflective practitioners, then the answer has to be 'yes'. This aspect of practice will be discussed more thoroughly in Chapter 5 – Time to work as a team.

When does assessment take place?

If assessment is a priority, then time must be found for it. Assessment should occur all the time and in some ways it does. All practitioners skilled in the art of assessment cannot help being observers. As soon as they walk into a room with children, they look and listen to what is going on. However, the information that is coming in all the time cannot possibly be held in the heads of the practitioners as there are too many other things going on. In addition, as Blenkin and Kelly (1992) argue, if the only assessment going on is that which occurs all the time, with practitioners assessing as they go, then the picture built up of the children will be a narrow one. For assessment to be worthwhile and meaningful, it needs to be planned. Also time needs to be set aside for assessment. Longer assessments will occur when children first start in a setting as practitioners get to know the children. Gradually shorter but more focused assessments will take place in order to build up a consistent and comprehensive picture of the child. The team in the setting also need to organise themselves so that there is a system for assessment whereby each child is assessed on a regular basis, preferably by different practitioners, so that different views of the child can occur and no child is missed out.

Spontaneous assessments are equally important. If a child demonstrates something that is noteworthy, then it should be acknowledged and recorded. Many practitioners find that as they engage in planned and focused assessments, then their ability to see and record in a more spontaneous way develops. Therefore, the answer to the question 'When should assessment take place?' is that it should be ongoing and planned over time but should also be spontaneous as the practitioner gets to know the child.

How do you assess?

As stated in the introduction to this chapter, there is a long tradition in early years education of observing and listening to children. Observation of young children is the key to assessment. Observation needs to be focused on the child and what they are doing so that practitioners can learn about their attitudes, interests, skills and knowledge. It can also be carried out by all adults involved in the life of the child.

Looking at children
Looking at children involves using all the senses and interpreting the information received in order to fully understand them. There are different ways to look at children and some will be more familiar and straightforward than others. Ways of looking discussed here are:

- narrative observations;
- observation schedules;
- photographs;
- videos;
- annotated work.

Narrative observations   We argued in the introduction to this chapter that there is a limited usefulness in check lists and tick sheets within the assessment process. We also argue for the usefulness of narrative records. 'A narrative approach will reflect the learning better than performance indicators' (Carr 2001: 93). Narrative records, where the practitioner records exactly what the child is doing and saying, will provide a wealth of information about the learning and development of the child being observed.

Narrative records built up over time provide a 'learning story' or 'learning journey' which provide clear evidence of a child's ongoing development, their attitudes, interests, skills and knowledge. This will present a fund of information on which to base the next steps in that journey.

A useful recording form is one that records initial background information such as name, date, start and finish time of the observation and then plenty of space to record the context and the observation. An example is given in Figure 3.1. This is a recording form that is used in the Foundation Stage in an infant school in the nursery and reception classes. Initially on starting in the setting every child is observed for 15 minutes two or three times a week. As the practitioners build up a picture of the child, 5-minute observations take place. Each month every child is observed for one day by both early years practitioners in the class: the teacher and the teaching assistant. The observations are then fed into records, the planning and shared with parents. The observation form provides the evidence to support an understanding of the child's development and learning as well as how the child interacts with the environment.

Observation schedules   As well as narrative observations, it is useful to use observation schedules which look at particular aspects of children's development. Two of the most useful observation forms, which provide information about the child's attitudes to learning, are the Child Involvement Schedule (Pascal *et al.* 1996) and the Well-being Scale (Laevers *et al.* 1994). The Child Involvement Schedule looks at how involved a child is in their learning and is a measure of the quality of the educational experiences with which the child is engaged. A child's involvement is measured on a five-point scale and repeated observations over time provide a wealth of information about the child's interests, attitudes and learning.

The Well-Being Scale looks at how happy a child is with the educational experiences being received. A child who is unhappy will not be learning as effectively as a child who is happy. Again, the measurement is on a five-point scale and repeated observations will provide useful information about a child.

Observation using photographs   Taking photographs provides powerful evidence for assessment. Photographs can easily be shared with and used by other adults. Photographs 'capture the moment' and as such need careful annotation so that the information contained within the photograph can be put into context. A single photograph of a child can convey information about their attitude, their interest at that moment and their skills. A sequence of photographs can convey the process of what the child is engaged in.

Observation Sheet

Child's name:...................
Date of birth:...................
Date of observation:...................
Start time:...................
Finish time:...................

The context:	What the child says:	What the child does:
Future action:		

Figure 3.1 Observation sheet used in the Foundation Stage in an infant school

The sequence of photographs that follows (Figure 3.2) demonstrates what can be learnt about a child engaged in a problem solving activity. Note the level of involvement and concentration, the thinking and physical skills involved in solving this particular problem and the joy at succeeding.

Photographs can be shared with parents to demonstrate their child's development and learning. They can provide points for discussion when there are questions or concerns. Parents can also be encouraged to take photographs and bring them into the setting to demonstrate children's development and learning at home. Parents need to be convinced of the value of taking and using photographs in the setting. The issue of confidentiality is, however, a serious one and permission must always be given to use photographs for other purposes.

Children can share in the taking and using of photographs by talking about a photograph they have taken. By providing a commentary to a photograph of themselves engaged in an activity, adults may learn about the child's thinking that underpins the activity, thereby gaining further information about the child.

Observation using video Videoing children at work can also provide valuable assessment material in much the same way as photographic evidence. Videoing young children is not as simple as photographing them and it needs to be a regular part of life in the setting otherwise children will 'perform' for the camera rather than engaging in their activities. Again video material can be shared with parents and video material can be brought in from home. This has been used very successfully at the Pen Green Early Years Centre in their work with children and families (Whalley 2001). For further discussion of this process see Chapter 4 – Time to develop home–school links.

Annotated work Finally, in this section we need to consider what looking at children's work can tell us. If we do not annotate children's work, it actually tells us very little. A collection of carefully annotated work, completed during different activities and within different contexts, can tell us a lot about a child's attitudes to their work and learning, their interests and their skills and knowledge. Figure 3.3 is a wax picture of a ladybird by a four-year-old. This was a part of an adult-initiated activity where the children were asked to draw pictures of insects. The children could choose their own media from a wide range of materials and choose what insect to draw. This child was particularly interested in ladybirds and, having free choice to work inside or outside, chose to go outside and find a ladybird to draw. The picture shows us the care and attention that the child has put into the piece of work, the physical skills in completing the work and the observational skills that the child is developing.

Observation is not only about looking but it is also about listening to children and it is through listening that children can be engaged in the assessment process.

1

2

3

4

Figure 3.2 Time taken to solve a problem and the obvious triumph when the solution has been reached

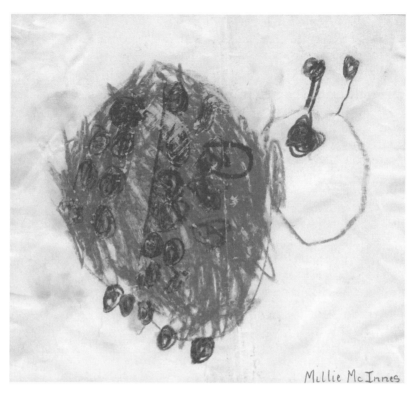

Millie McInnes

Figure 3.3 Wax picture of a ladybird by Millie, aged four years

Listening to children

Listening to children means that we take them seriously and we involve them in the assessment process. Clark *et al.* (2003) discuss the research into ways of listening to children and the impact that this can have on children and practitioners. Some points that are worth noting are that children's self-esteem can be raised through having their views taken seriously and that they develop skills and understanding through talking about their experiences. Practitioners reported that listening to children made them think and opened their eyes to children's thinking and understanding. Parents also had their eyes opened to the abilities of their children and this enabled them to raise their expectations concerning what their children were capable of. There are a variety of techniques for listening to children. The most familiar approach is that of child conferencing but other, more innovatory techniques may be employed such as using cameras and role-play (Clark and Moss 2001).

Child conferencing   Child conferencing means talking to children or interviewing them about their likes, dislikes. It involves talking about what they think they are good at and any other subjects of interest. Talking to children as a part of the assessment process often brings the assessment alive for parents as they see their child's voice on paper. It also tells the practitioner crucial information about the child's attitudes to learning or aspects of learning. The child who says, 'I like reading and I am good at it. I also like playing with dolls and the doll's house' conveys information about their interests, attitudes to learning and the provision in the setting. Clark and Moss (2001) cite considerations that need to be made when engaging in child conferencing: think about the setting, be prepared to move around as you talk, be sensitive to children's needs during the conference and give children time to make their responses.

Cameras and role-play Children can be highly proficient in using cameras once shown how to use them. Children can use cameras to take photographs of people, areas and objects. Talking about the photographs they take allows them to open up and again reveal their attitudes, interests, skills and knowledge about themselves, the setting and others. Using toy figures to explain their experiences in the setting, through role-play, often enables children to talk about personal details in a way that may be difficult in an interview situation. Again, with careful attention to detail practitioners may learn about children as they weave a story with their toy figures.

These different ways of looking at and listening to children provide evidence that can be put together to form a complete picture of the child. As previously stated, this takes time but it is time well spent.

Time for using the evidence from assessment

In the introduction to this chapter we established the need for assessment and in the previous section we discussed how we use time to assess young children. Now we turn our attention to how we use the evidence from assessment over time. It is no use collecting evidence of children's development and learning without doing something meaningful with this evidence. In this section we will look at how we share the evidence from assessment with others.

Time for dialogue with others

As already discussed, all the adults who engage with the child need to be involved in the assessment process through constant dialogue. Dialogue is a two-way process whereby each party voices their thoughts and opinions and is listened to. The dialogue or conversation may involve many different issues and will occur at different stages of a child's time in the Foundation Stage. It may also take many forms, including verbal and written dialogue. Meaningful dialogue takes time and has to be planned for, so that it is worthwhile.

Verbal dialogue

Verbal dialogue should be an ongoing process and one that occurs with parents at the beginning and end of a session. Talking to a parent or carer about the activities their child has taken part in, what the child might have said and any significant achievements are all a part of reporting evidence from the assessment process. Likewise, the parent or carer reporting to practitioners any interesting or significant information can contribute to the assessment process and help build up a picture of the child. Practitioners need to organise their time so that it is a part of the everyday routine. This may occur through one practitioner being with the children and one being available for talking to parents and carers where there are two practitioners working together. If that is not possible, and in many classes it isn't, ways need to be found for children to be independent to enable the practitioner to have that time for dialogue, for example, self-registration followed by planning with parents.

Conversations also need to take place with other professionals that the child has had contact with. These may include practitioners from other Foundation Stage settings or professionals from other agencies that may work with the child. Dialogue may be informal, for example, when a childminder brings a child for a nursery session and the nursery practitioner and childminder share information on the child's well-being during the morning. It may, however, be more formal, for example, a health visitor verbally reporting to a Foundation Stage practitioner on the outcome of a hearing assessment.

Written dialogue

Written dialogue may take many different forms from structured school reports and the Foundation Stage Profile (QCA 2003) to more informal learning journeys and documentation. As with verbal dialogue, written dialogue should be two-way with parents, carers and other professionals having the opportunity to either respond to or contribute to the process.

Report writing   Report writing occurs at different points during a child's time during the Foundation Stage and is drawn from the assessment evidence collected prior to the report being written. Usually during the course of an academic year reports will be written during each of the three terms. The first term's report will use the evidence collected from initial assessments to discuss how the child has settled into the setting and aspects of the child's development are usually framed around the areas of the curriculum detailed in *The Curriculum Guidance for the Foundation Stage* (QCA 2000) as well as a section on the child as a learner. Parents will have an opportunity to respond to the report in written form. The second report will detail progress so far and the final report will be a discussion of what the child has achieved during the course of the year, drawing upon the evidence collected from all the assessments. Again the report will be written using the same format as before and parents will have the chance to respond. Children should also have an opportunity to contribute to the process either by writing themselves or having someone scribing their opinions, their likes, dislikes and interests. Copies of reports may go to other practitioners at times of transition, for example, a report from a playgroup going to a reception class. Again, report writing is time-consuming. It has to be done and should prove to be useful to the recipient if it provides a meaningful picture of the child.

Foundation Stage Profile   The Foundation Stage Profile (QCA 2003) should be filled in during the reception year and completed by the end of that year. It builds on the curriculum guidance and practitioners should use the evidence from observations to complete it. The profile is set out as a set of 13 assessment scales drawn from the early learning goals (QCA 2000) and each scale has nine points. Every term practitioners should use the evidence from observations to make judgements as to whether a child has achieved each point on the scale. There are also opportunities for practitioners to record written evidence and for parents and children to contribute to the profile. How often is this profile completed at the end of a child's time in a setting and in a hurry?

There has been considerable discussion and debate concerning the Foundation Stage Profile. It has been heavily criticised for the amount of time it takes to complete (Ofsted 2004a) and for the fact that it is viewed by many practitioners to be nothing more than a glorified tick-list (Wragg 2003). Many practitioners have stated that the profile is fine as a summative record but it needs something more substantial to go alongside it. For those practitioners who have developed additional material and make observation a daily part of their practice, it is not an onerous document to complete. What then becomes more worrying, is how it will be used on transition to Key Stage 1. Hopefully colleagues in Key Stage 1 will use it as the starting point for their work with children. For those children who have not achieved the early learning goals, there is a chance to work with the curriculum guidance for the Foundation Stage alongside the National Curriculum. At present this does not, however, appear to be the case (Ofsted 2004a).

Learning journeys   As stated above, many practitioners view the Foundation Stage Profile as not being enough on its own. For those practitioners, keeping a collection of evidence drawn from observations, children's dialogue, photographs, video and work during their time in the Foundation Stage is a necessary part of their practice. This collection may be termed a child's learning journey (Carr 2001). Parents, carers, other practitioners and children may all contribute to this learning journey which is then taken forward by the child at points of transition. For the practitioner who receives the child, this collection of assessment evidence provides a far more powerful and complete picture of the child than any other form of assessment evidence. Parents are also confident that through the learning journey evidence from assessment has been collated to give a complete and comprehensive view of their child. Parents can recognise the voice of their child in the dialogue and know that practitioners are building upon the skills, knowledge, understanding and attitudes displayed by their child. The following examples are from a child's learning journey through the Foundation Stage in an infant school.

A statement from the child is recorded followed by the adult's comment regarding assessment of the child and then the next steps for the child are identified.

Child: 'Georgia sat in my chair and I asked her to move but she didn't.'
Adult: Millie is attempting to independently resolve conflict.
Next steps: To persevere with dealing with conflict and to try to resolve situations before asking an adult for help.
Child: 'You need to leave spaces after your words.'
Adult: Millie is aware of the structure of a sentence.
Next steps: To attempt to write sentences in her own independent writing.
Child: 'That puppet must be from a hot country. She doesn't have any shoes on.'
Next steps: To increase her knowledge of a variety of cultures, countries and festivals.

Documentation   In the first section of this chapter, documentation, as a means of assessment, was introduced. The argument has already been put forward that informal assessment, although desirable, is not going on all the time. Documentation is, however, an example of assessment that is built into the design of the Reggio Emilia programme and without it the nature of the curriculum would be very different. Documentation is discussed by Forman and Fyfe (in Edwards *et al.* 1998: 245) as an extension of a display. 'The passage from display to documentation travels the path from informing to educating and therefore changes the teacher's perspective from observing children to studying children.'

Documentation is focused on groups of children rather than on individuals. It raises questions about children's thinking and helps to assess the appropriateness of the learning experiences. Documentation is a part of reflective teaching in the Reggio Emilia programme originating from northern Italy that is based on a sound theory of social constructivist knowledge. Children are helped to understand their ways of working, their communication with one another and the negotiations that they have with others. Children's ideas and theories are elicited and supported and they are encouraged to talk about what they already know about a topic. Documenting or recording this knowledge allows the teacher to study children rather than teach them and through studying be able to learn with them.

Children are responsible for designing much of the way forward in a Reggio project and by talking about their work they are entering into what Forman and Fyfe (in Edwards *et al.* 1998: 240) describe as 'the discourse of prediction and explanation'. *Design* refers to children being able to communicate their ideas through graphic representation; often drawing. *Discourse* is not just talking but demands an understanding of what is being said and the opportunity to confront others and accept different perspectives. *Documentation* is a means of explaining children's learning. It is not used to describe individual learning but to provide evidence of group learning and the educational intentions, progress and outcomes of different activities. Documentation should be available for open discussion with parents and all adults concerned with the education and the care of the children. Some of the documentation will be used as entries in portfolios or continuous records of the development of individuals.

The use of portfolios is another positive aspect of informal assessment in the Reggio Emilia approach. These are built up over time and contain drawings, photographs, diagrams and a variety of other evidence of children's thinking and developing understanding. The contents define the chronological development of individual children and provide a very useful form of assessment. These are successful if they provide a clear picture of the child's development across all areas of learning, if the child has ownership of them and if they are kept up to date.

Assessment has been shown to have many variations. In this chapter we have explored some of the variations and highlighted the importance of sincere and accurate records of children's learning. Time is shown to be a key feature in accomplishing this aim. Not all ways of assessing children will be appropriate to every setting, nor will all practitioners feel comfortable or experienced enough to take all ways of assessing on board. Teaching and learning are dynamic processes and openness to new ideas will lead to more effective practice. In the next chapter we consider the importance of time in establishing home–school partnerships.

CHAPTER 4

Time to develop a home–school partnership

Imagine early years centres where all staff are beginning to be assertive; self-critical and supportively critical of others . . . Centres in which the adults, parents and staff are rigorous thinkers, focused and analytical . . . where the work is rooted in the local community but staff also reach out, make their views known and challenge local and central Government over important issues.

(Whalley 2001: ix)

Why we need time to make home–school links

The Curriculum Guidance for the Foundation Stage (QCA 2000: 9) suggests that, 'Parents are children's first and most enduring educators.' What do we understand by this statement? As well as parents, a range of other important carers may look after children. These might include grandparents, childminders or nursery staff. Each of these adults will contribute to children's experience and help them to establish expectations and enthusiasm for learning. Do we understand the contribution that parents and carers could make to the education of their own children and to the school community? Do we take time to recognise the bank of experiences, skills and knowledge that children bring to a setting? Do we really think that it is necessary to find out about the child's world at home?

In this chapter we raise questions about the role that parents play in their children's early education and offer some suggestions as to how to use time to set up and sustain meaningful links between the child's world at home and the world of the setting. As the chapter unfolds, we hope that we make a distinction between *involving* parents in the setting and developing a true *partnership* between the adults and parents.

Involvement of parents may include:

- doing tasks such as washing paint pots or mending books;
- contributing particular skills such as playing the guitar or telling stories;
- attending courses and meetings that inform them about the curriculum;

- being part of a group who hear children read or work in some other way in the classroom;

- taking part in parent/teacher organisations and contributing to fundraising.

A *partnership* with parents must include *involvement* but further requires:

- educators to visit homes and continually share information about home and school with parents;

- parents to get to know the practitioners and understand the aims for the child's education, through regular discussion of the child's progress and relating of anecdotes and incidents that help to build a picture of the whole child;

- possible opportunities for parents to work at their own level on projects that will enhance their skills and self-esteem and benefit their children (Pen Green: Whalley 2001);

- parents and teacher to have a two-way relationship where each feels that there is time to consider the needs of the child.

What is the difference between the two suggested ways of interacting? The problem with the simple *involvement* model is that usually the educators remain in control and are able to make judgements as to which parents can contribute and in what way. A *partnership* model, on the other hand, requires an explicit understanding of the contribution that *all* adults are making to their child's care and education. It is a model that must be built on trust and true dialogue. It is a model that takes time. *The Curriculum Guidance for the Foundation Stage* (QCA 2000) has highlighted key issues for early education and care, through its principles and areas of learning. This has led to a more organised curriculum and often, sadly, a more formal programme than is appropriate for young children. Over the years local authorities had traditionally framed their own educational objectives for the care and education of young children. Settings operated with a high degree of autonomy. Most practitioners were not encouraged to listen to parents, to discuss the professional practice in the setting or to involve parents in the decisions that were being made about their children's education. The early years *policy* was very much about 'we (the practitioners) know best!'

In the 1960s and 1970s there were pockets of excellence among settings where high quality learning experiences were offered and adults took time to keep records of children's sustained interest and monitor their development. Practitioners from all over the world visited these settings and took ideas back to their own countries. Investigative projects were set up through bodies such as the Schools Council and evidence of good practice was published (Parry and Archer 1975). In unsatisfactory settings the practice was poor with little or no evaluation or reflection. However, in most settings at this time there was little evidence of any time given to parents or any value placed on children's experience at home.

Schools often denied parents the right to 'educate' their children. 'Don't teach him to read or write, we can do that at school.' 'Oh, he can read, can he? Well, we will have to teach him our way now.'

The important role that parents should play in the education of children began to be recognised in the 1970s and gathered momentum in the 1980s. 'A shift in attitude to parental involvement in education has certainly been a welcome feature of recent years' (Wolfendale 1989: vi). Prior to this period 'parents remained as an untapped source of strength to the school' (ibid.: vii). Most early provision catered for children who were caught in the poverty trap. Evidence was coming from the USA that there was a benefit to the development of young children when intervention programmes were set up to compensate for perceived disadvantage. 'It is clear from reports of both *Headstart* projects in the USA and the Educational Priority Areas in England in the sixties and seventies that many of the practitioners at that time equated poverty with cultural deprivation' (Whalley 1994: 106). Attempts were made to alter the perceptions of child rearing that parents held and to establish middle-class values. It was expected that inequality would be eradicated through educational provision and care for the children and educational programmes for parents. The versions of the American programmes established in this country had the same *deficit* ideals – it was the parents who had to change! Involvement of parents was to be commended but the chosen style of involvement was proving to be less satisfactory.

It is easy to be critical when considering the historical perspective of an issue. The programmes in the USA and in this country were established in good faith. Children's failure to thrive, for whatever reason, needed to be addressed. More than 30 years later we should be able to report on the positive progress of a partnership with parents. We should be able to take for granted that parents have a right to make a range of contributions. It was found, however, that real change could not be made nor progress established when the partnership between parents and the *establishment* was an unequal one. Progress would never be made while there was uneasiness on the part of the educators as to how to share their knowledge and understanding. In the case of the parents, the problem lay in a lack of understanding of what contribution they could make and how that contribution could be valued.

The very influential research by Tizard and Hughes (1984) and Wells (1996) indicated that practitioners needed to find out more about children's lives outside the setting. They needed to acknowledge that children had a variety of skills appropriate to their homes and that the home needed to be reflected in children's experience in the setting. These findings were reflected in the experience of Margy Whalley. In 1983 she set up the Pen Green Centre, for under-fives, in Corby. From the outset the role of parents in their children's education was seen as important. Time was given initially to mothers, many of whom had very low self-esteem and felt that they had 'failed'. Whalley talks about 'educators missing the point'

(Whalley 1994: 107). The importance of the parental contribution had been under-estimated with practitioners failing to 'appreciate what parents were doing for children and their aspirations for their children' (ibid.). The setting has flourished and has attracted international interest.

The results of a five-year research project set up in 1995 have been disseminated with training programmes that followed delivered by parents and staff. A vision for the future was articulated by Whalley (2001), at the start of this chapter. This vision has not been widely realised outside the Pen Green Early Years Centre although, once again there are pockets of excellence and a general feeling that parental partnership should be an ideal. It is important to understand that a partnership with parents requires an investment of time. Table 4.1 is adapted from Whalley (ibid.: 20). It provides an excellent starting point for the reflective thinking necessary for staff and parents if children's emotional lives are to be valued and provision made for cognitive challenge and independent learning.

Table 4.1 Aims for successful partnership

Aims for Children	Aims for Parents	Aims for Educators
To value them as individuals	To help them to observe, understand and value what the children are learning at home	For all staff to be active practitioners who can debate, reflect and articulate theory and practice
To help to raise their self-esteem		
To provide stimulating, holistic curriculum experiences	To develop their confidence in their skills and competencies	For all staff to develop genuine dialogue with parents
To consider the younger siblings and the relevance of the early years programme to them	To encourage an equal partnership and active involvement in their child's setting	For all staff to share the knowledge and expertise of parents and staff as widely as possible
	To encourage a two-way relationship with educators where value is given to contributions	
	To give all parents an accessible route into involvement with their children's development	

The success of the parental partnership in the Pen Green Early Years Centre has been the result of very hard work. It is easy to read the entries on Table 4.1 and adopt them for a policy for parental partnership. However, to enable the rhetoric to become reality requires a huge investment in time.

How we use time to develop a home–school partnership

Now that we have advocated the need for an effective, working partnership we must identify how we use our time to make these links and engage in partnership. In doing this we must ask, who is responsible for making these links? Should this be left to teachers within the setting or should all practitioners, including students, be involved in this process? We must also ask what purpose there is in making links. It is very easy to ask parents and carers about a child's daily life without really listening. It is very easy to ask questions to which we think we already know the answers. If we don't ask serious questions and take the answers seriously, then are we guilty of wasting parents' and carers' time? We should also consider when to make home–school links. Is this a process that starts when the child enters the setting? Is it ongoing or is it an activity that is confined to certain times of the year? Finally, how we engage with parents and carers and make meaningful home–school links will affect the quality and usefulness of the partnership.

Who makes home–school links?

We would argue that it is the responsibility of everyone who works in the setting to make links with parents and carers. In early years settings, where a key worker system is in place, each practitioner will be allocated a number of children to work with directly. It will then be the key worker's role to make links with the parents and carers of those children and share relevant information with the rest of the team. In settings where there is no such system in place, the lines of responsibility become more blurred. Teachers often believe that it is their role to make links but often that is not practical. For example, in a nursery class of 52 children attending part-time, the commitment would be too great for one person. Or it may be inappropriate, for example, when some parents have a better rapport with other members of staff. The teacher or leader of the team needs, however, to have a shared general understanding of all the children's lives at home.

The issue of some practitioners getting on better with some parents and carers than others can be a difficult one. It is often a situation that calls for shared responsibility and time being allocated for all practitioners to have periods when they are available for parents. This may be achieved through practitioners taking turns to start and end the day so that each person is available at those times for parents and carers. It is also important for practitioners to meet and share information about the home–school links that are being made so that there is a team understanding of the needs of the families.

In the introduction to this section we questioned whether students should be involved in home–school partnerships. We would argue that students do need to be involved in this process. If students are to develop as effective early years practitioners, they need experience of engaging with parents and carers before they have daily responsibility after qualification. Nurse and Headington (in David 1999) stated that within initial teacher training programmes this was a neglected area. This is still the case today as newly qualified teachers state that they feel poorly equipped to work with parents (Lee 2004). In early years settings there may be students from a range of disciplines. They may be involved by having two or three children for whom they are expected to keep in-depth profiles. This should include finding out about the child's home background, their likes, dislikes and interests at home and at school and talking to parents and carers. Students may be given the opportunity to write interim end-of-term or end-of-year reports and then report information to parents.

The involvement of all staff in the home lives of young children raises issues of integrity, confidentiality and sensitivity. As well as practitioners and students, there may be parent helpers. Helpers may see or learn information about children which they may then pass on to parents. Having parents and other helpers working in the setting is a powerful way of fostering home–school links and will be discussed in more detail later in the chapter. They will, however, need to be a part of the team and to understand the approach that is adopted to the home–school partnership by other team members.

What links do we make between home and school?

'In the early years, home and community culture are extremely influential on learning and children do not leave their culture behind them as they come in through the doors of the setting' (Devereux and Miller 2003: 89). Practitioners need to find out and understand the culture that children bring with them to settings. That can only happen by taking time to be interested, asking questions and valuing the answers that are given. Parents and carers need to be treated with trust and feel that there is genuine respect for home and family life. This will not happen when spurious questions are asked or practitioners do not operate in an atmosphere of mutual understanding.

A positive model for this way of working comes from the Reggio Emilia approach to early years education. Leask, writing in Abbott and Nutbrown (2001: 44), details her experience of being the parent of a child in the Reggio system. The questions were not just routine ones such as, 'How did he behave?' or 'What does he like and dislike?' They included:

> How did he behave when he was tired? How did he like being held? What did he like doing? What sort of character was he? What sort of routine did we have at home? What type of home life did we have – quiet and regulated, or full of comings and goings?

These questions are detailed, take time to answer properly and provide important information. These questions were used to form a biography of her child, which was then documented and displayed so that all those working in, and visiting, the setting knew about her child and the best ways to engage with him.

When do we make home–school links?

Do we make home–school links when children start in a setting or earlier? Surely if we want to truly understand the culture in which a child lives, we need to start before a child enters a setting. This should begin with practitioners gaining knowledge of the local community and the easiest way to do this is to walk around the local area. By doing this, it is possible to see the type of housing in which children coming to the setting live, and the play opportunities available, and these can be very different, depending on the area. For example, children in a small rural village may have different accommodation and a range of play opportunities not available to those children living in a large inner city area. Similarly children from the inner city may have a greater understanding of traffic flow and crossing a main road (Figure 4.1).

Visiting the local area provides opportunities to look at local facilities – the types of shops and the food items that they sell, the local places where people in the community gather, places of worship, sports and play facilities. It may be possible to identify places of employment and to gain an understanding of the kind of lives people lead. For example, children living near Longleat Safari Park, in Wiltshire, where many of their parents work, gain an understanding of the lives and life-cycles of exotic animals and use language and concepts that would be inexplicable to many city children. Similarly, children who live in a mixed race community may be familiar with a close communal and probably religious experience. They may attend Koran school from an early age and be familiar with fragrant and spicy cooking. There will always be those children to whom we attribute a label who will surprise us with their unsuspected experiences.

Taking time to engage in this initial fact-finding will provide background knowledge to the lives of children attending the setting and a base from which to make home–school links. It also shows a willingness and commitment to understand the local community, and ensure that meaningful conversations can take place between practitioners and parents and carers.

In our careers in teaching we have gained wide-ranging information about children's backgrounds. One evening, a teacher on an early years course led a seminar where she discussed a holiday project with three- and four-year-olds. She had used a map of the world and parents were encouraged to bring in artefacts gathered from their holidays. Only one child, in her class, had not been to Europe and many had visited the United States and Asia. The range of artefacts brought into the setting covered obvious interests and some indicated special interests and important knowledge. She gave an example of a family who contributed their collection of indigenous musical instruments and discovered the family's intense interest in music that was also very important to their child. Williams (2003) describes having discussed fishing with a child who was finding it difficult to make relationships in the setting. His father was approached and willingly

Figure 4.1   What do we know about the opportunities available to children in their home areas?

brought in his fishing gear and magazines. From that moment on the child gained recognition from his peers and the father contributed to a school environment where he might otherwise have felt out of place. These are only examples of the varied ways in which partnerships can be fuelled. Making home–school links is a continuous process throughout a child's time in the setting and during times of transition. A partnership with parents should be positive and long lasting. In the Reggio Emilia experience, in northern Italy, there is a reliance on the loyalty and commitment of parents, years after their children have left the schools.

How do we make home–school links?

In the section above we identified that the process of making home–school links begins before the child enters the setting. Having gained knowledge of the local community, practitioners also need to get to know the children before they start in the setting.

Initial visits to make home–school links

If a child attends a local playgroup or other pre-school setting, then a visit should be made to meet the practitioner in that setting and to see the child at play. Knowledge should be gained about the setting: the routine during the session, the activities and resources available, the curriculum on offer and the quality of adult–child relationships. Conversations can also take place to determine the type of activities the child enjoys during the session, which resources are preferred and how they are used and how the child responds to other children and adults. It may also be beneficial for the visiting practitioners to join in the session, perhaps taking a story time, so that the child can get to know the new practitioner on familiar ground.

Another powerful way to make initial home–school links is through taking time to make a home visit. Hurst (in Blenkin and Kelly 1996) outlines how valuable this can be for the child, parents and practitioner and how this forms the basis of a secure two-way communication process. During a home visit, practitioners can discuss with parents the school's perspective on learning and development and parents can introduce practitioners to the needs and characteristics of their child. Practitioners can also introduce children to the setting on their home territory by taking a scrapbook with photographs of children at play in the setting or other interesting information to arouse the child's interest and curiosity. This will enable the child to become familiar with the activities that may take place and the possibilities that the environment has to offer. Taking a photograph of the child when going on a home visit can also be useful and provide a starting point for initial conversations, 'Do you remember when I visited you at home and played with you and your brother in the garden?' It is not always possible to make home visits and some parents and possibly staff may not want to take part. Initially this should be respected. If, however, the importance of a partnership with parents is fundamental, then staff training must help to allay fears and to highlight the positive outcomes for both children and adults. Working with parents who are resistant to attempts to make home–school links is discussed later in the chapter.

As well as the practitioner visiting the setting the child is currently attending and making a home visit, time needs to be organised for the child to visit the new setting, preferably more than once. There needs to be an opportunity for the child to meet the other children who will be in the setting, to experience the environment and to engage in activities and use resources. Parents should also be given the opportunity to visit the setting with their child, in order to provide security for the child, and also security for the adult so that they have knowledge about the setting their child is going to attend. Alongside visit days for children and adults, there also needs to be information sessions for parents. Ideally, information sessions should give parents and carers much of the relevant information they need to know about the setting. It should also give them an opportunity to meet all the adults with whom their child will come into contact; not only early years practitioners but also health professionals such as the school nurse, the health visitor and the speech and language therapist.

Nurturing home–school links

Settling children into an early years setting needs time but, if managed sensitively, can greatly benefit children, parents and practitioners. How best to settle children is one issue that is keenly debated:

1 Should all children start at once or in small groups?

2 If children have a staggered start, how is that best managed?

3 Should the oldest children start first or the youngest?

Many settings start children in small groups as this gives children and practitioners time to get to know one another. This also enables practitioners, parents and carers to talk to one another and learn about each other. This is a good time to nurture the tentative links already made through initial visits and meetings. How children are organised into small groups to begin their time in the setting is an issue for early years teams to discuss. Whatever is decided should be based on sound principles and should be clearly articulated to parents.

Another issue for discussion by early years teams is that of children bringing well-loved resources into the setting from home. Many practitioners do not allow this to happen or they ensure that children are not allowed to play with their favourite item while in the setting. Being told to put teddy in the 'going home box' is a typical response. Why should this be? Allowing children to bring in favourite items from home and playing with them and sharing them with their newly made friends in the setting provides them with security and gives them confidence to communicate with others. It also provides a bridge between home and school and enables conversations and learning to take place about home and school. Parents will also feel confident that their children are respected and their home life is valued and they feel more able to open up and talk to staff. When this happens, then real understanding between home and school has started. The following statements are taken from a child's 'learning journey' or log of significant events and practitioners' responses. They were recorded during the Foundation Stage in an infant school and demonstrate what the child said and the response and understanding of the staff.

Child's comment: 'We had a parcel delivered to our house and there was some clothes for me and some for Sophie and all my clothes fitted me, they did.'

Adult's observation: Millie is willing to share her home experiences.

Child's comment: '*Ness the Nurse* is my favourite book, it is so funny.'

Adult's observation: Millie said every word as the adult read the story and was able to identify all the children's names in the print. She likes to share books at home.

Child's comment: 'My mum has a brush like that, it's for cleaning the cat's bowl.'

Adult's observation: Millie is able to make comparisons between objects found at home and at school.

As well as finding time for sharing and talking, time also needs to be found to observe parents and carers interacting with their children at the beginning and end of sessions. Watching how children separate from and greet their adults can inform practitioners about the values and attitudes within the home and the verbal and non-verbal forms of communication used. This information can then be used as the starting point for future discussions and to inform the way in which practitioners work with children. An example might be to use familiar language when comforting an child who is upset.

Home–school links should involve written communication. A home–school book or diary is a good starting point especially for those parents who are unable to visit regularly. Setting up a parents' board either outside the room or in a central place is also useful. The board may have the weekly timetable, activities and other informative notices pinned up. It may also be a place where parents can share information and place their own notices informing other parents and carers of items of interest. Take care though that you understand the literacy difficulties of parents who cannot read through lack of understanding or through impaired sight. These parents will need other forms of communication.

A board may also be set up for children to place any work from home. This is a successful way to value what children do at home. The board can be set up at children's height with drawings, writing, photographs and any other material that children wish to share. Empowering children in this way raises their confidence and self-esteem by allowing others to see what is important to them. It also provides a talking point for children and practitioners about the types of activities that go on at home as well as a possible starting point for conversations with parents and carers about additional, appropriate activities for young children.

Finally, activities need to be developed which help nurture home–school links and enable children to build up confidence about themselves and to share their home lives with others in the setting. One valuable artefact is the 'special box'. Each day during the first few weeks in the setting each child takes it in turn to take home the 'special box'. The box is empty and the child chooses a small number of special objects from home to put in it to bring in the next day and share with everyone else. Objects might include a toy, a photograph of siblings or a comfort object. The objects and their significance to the child should be discussed by the group.

Sustaining and developing home–school links

Having spent time on initiating and looking for creative ways to promote home–school links, it is time to look at ways to sustain and extend these links. Parents differ in the amount of contact they wish to have with their child's setting and with the practitioners who work with their child. Different families need different approaches to a partnership (Whalley 2001). Whatever the approach, however, it needs to be clear to parents that they are welcome in the setting, that learning that occurs in the home is valued and that learning that occurs in the setting should be shared and followed up in the home (Hurst, in Blenkin and Kelly 1996). A review of the literature by Desforges and Abouchaar (2003) shows that there are many forms of ongoing parental involvement and that this can have a positive influence on children's learning and development.

Welcoming parents into the setting

A warm welcome provides the start for involvement and partnership. Parents should be invited into the setting to share in their children's learning and development on a regular basis. Finding different formats that enable parents to understand the experiences their children are having is challenging. The most obvious way is to hold open evenings/times focused on different aspects of the curriculum. Information is shared with parents and examples of work and activities and children's responses to them can be shown.

As well as informal opportunities to visit their children's settings, there should also be a variety of interesting occasions for parents to understand more about their children's education. There should be opportunities to attend:

- open days where adults and children can work together, with a range of materials, in an informal and unthreatening atmosphere;
- workshops with a particular focus, such as an area of the curriculum or a current project;
- workshops that focus on areas of interest for parents.

This first-hand experience should enable parents to experience learning in the same way as their children. Meetings with members of the team and other professionals, for example, the health visitor and speech and language therapist, are also valuable. These meetings should allow the parents and the professionals to engage in meaningful dialogue.

Many practitioners do not feel comfortable with these ways of working and need to develop confidence to interact with parents. However, if we wish to engage with parents and make real home–school links, then we must take the time to challenge ourselves as professionals and develop our own attitudes, skills and knowledge. It is also important that parents are valued not only for their expertise as parents but also for the skills that they may be able to offer in the setting (Devereux and Miller 2003). All parents have skills that can be shared with the children. Being open with parents allows practitioners to learn about the culture of the home and to find out more about children's starting points for learning. Parents with particular skills, for example, carpentry, may come in and work with children at the woodwork benches. Parents with knowledge and experience of different cultures may share this through cookery sessions with children or playing with the children in the role-play area.

As well as inviting parents into the setting, it is also important to invite members of the community. Local shopkeepers, policemen or religious leaders all have much to say to young children. Their experiences will broaden the children's understanding of the wider environment in which they live and broaden the practitioners' understanding of the community in which they work. As well as building on practitioners' initial understanding of the local community, it will help to dispel misunderstandings and enable them to work with parents and carers from a more informed viewpoint.

A two-way communication process

In order to sustain and develop home–school links, two-way communication is crucial. Finding out information from home and using this to inform practice, as already discussed, is important. Inviting parents in to help with understanding the diversity of culture and to offer their skills to foster children's development is also important.

The dialogue between practitioners and parents must be two-way. There has to be an extension from the setting to the school. This could be parents creating a 'home learning environment or HLE', as cited in Desforges and Abouchaar (2003), through a range of learning-related provision. Both Melhuish *et al.* (2001) and Siraj-Blatchford *et al.* (2002) conclude from their research that where staff and parents share educational information and parents work to sustain this at home through an HLE, there is increased co-operation, confidence, sociability and better development of children's thinking. Ways to foster this include weekly written reports to parents, detailing activities their children have been engaging in, taking books home to share and games to play. An extension of written reports is the practice of documentation seen in settings in the town of Reggio Emilia and discussed in Chapter 3.

Another form of communication and again one used in the process of documentation is that of photographing children and sharing this with parents and carers. In one particular setting the team focus on a particular child each week and during the week photographs are taken of the child engaged in different activities and working with different children and adults. Photographs are put together to form a montage of the child's week and practitioners and the child add comments about the photographs. This is presented to the family as a snapshot of the child in the setting. From this, parents may understand what their child enjoys doing and the possibilities for continuing to develop these interests at home.

Photographic evidence can also be used to encourage parents' interest in what children enjoy in school or conversely to allay parental concern regarding a child's progress. The photograph in Figure 4.2 was taken in response to a parent's question concerning her child's insistence that she had no friends and no one would play with her. This photograph showed the child in question involved in a lengthy period of make-believe play with her best friend. This was one of a sequence of photographs detailing the development of the play during a morning session.

Figure 4.2   Millie and George working together

Another way of developing two-way communication is by using a video camera in the setting and sharing the videotapes with parents. Many practitioners, however, may feel uncomfortable with using video cameras. Some consider the use of cameras as an infringement of children's rights. As with any form of photography, clear boundaries need to be set in terms of material to be videoed, with discussion relating to what is recorded, and the feelings and wishes of the children. Parents can reserve the right to prevent their children from being photographed. As we have said before, they will hopefully come to see the value of capturing 'moments in time' to further work with the children. For a fuller discussion of the importance of boundary setting in this work, see Whalley (2001). Once guidelines have been set and observed, sharing and discussing video material can be a powerful way for parents to fully understand the work of the setting and their child within the setting. It is also enlightening for practitioners to gain the parents' perspective on what their child is doing, as nuances of body language can be picked up by parents and a different understanding of the child may emerge. Whalley (ibid.) reports that parents say that they learn about their children from this way of working, that they respond to their children differently having observed practitioners working with their children, and that they select different resources for their children at home.

Difficulty in engaging with parents

There are many reasons why some parents do not want to get involved in making links between home and school. Families may be from backgrounds where they have not been expected to take any part in the formal world of the school. They may speak other languages and feel unable to enter into the communication necessary to make and sustain links. They may have problems with literacy that can prevent them from taking up opportunities to engage fully in the life of the setting. They may have had bad experiences themselves during their time in school and feel threatened by the environment. There is also the attitude that schools and practitioners know best and therefore should be left to get on with the job of educating their child. Finally, there can be practical reasons why families do not get involved. Some of these may include both parents working full-time, making it difficult to attend the school during the day, or responsibility for younger siblings. Offering different times of the day or the evening when parents may visit, having a crèche for younger siblings or, as already discussed, using home–school books may prove to be useful suggestions to overcome some of these practical difficulties.

Difficulties with engaging with parents from other backgrounds and with other languages may also be overcome. Devereux and Miller (2003) outline a variety of strategies to enable parents to address these particular challenges. Suggestions include having resources which acknowledge cultural heritage and language so that parents are reassured that the intentions of the setting are genuine. Engaging an adult worker or helper who shares the same culture or language so that parents have a point of contact will be important. In addition, it is suggested that there should be opportunities for parents to improve their literacy and oral skills, where necessary, in a friendly environment. This will also apply to those for whom English is a second language.

Probably the hardest group of parents to reach are those who have had bad educational experiences themselves, who do not wish to get involved for the feelings it engenders and so leave practitioners to get on with it. Arnold, in Whalley (2001), discusses ways to involve this group and suggests strategies for involving them, based on personal experience of the Pen Green project on parental involvement. She discusses the importance of genuine respect and liking for children and their parents and the art of true communication which enables parents to feel secure and to open up. She also discusses the importance of empathising and acknowledging parents' true feelings about situations and discussing this, while helping parents find solutions to handling them. Finally, she outlines the need to take on board suggestions made by parents and to act upon them for the good of parents, the children and practitioners.

Home–school links and transition to Key Stage 1

Transition from the Foundation Stage to Key Stage 1 is a time of uncertainty and anxiety for both children and parents. It is also a time when the strength of the home–school links, which have been built up during the Foundation Stage, are tested to the full as the most fragile links can easily be broken if the transition does not go smoothly. To ensure that this transition goes well, it is necessary to involve parents and to meet their needs as well as the needs of their children.

Obviously practitioners in both Key Stages need to work together so that information about the child is communicated. Practitioners in Key Stage 1 need to visit the children in the Foundation Stage and children need to visit their new class in Key Stage 1 in much the same way as when children enter the Foundation Stage. Children going home and talking about their experiences of visiting and being visited provide the starting point for parents to become involved in the process.

Ofsted (2004a), in its report on the transition from Reception to Key Stage 1, outlines what is necessary for effective parental involvement during this transition time:

- holding meetings for parents so that they can meet the Key Stage 1 team is important so that new people can be identified and information can be relayed;
- enabling parents to visit the new teacher in the new class is also useful as the environment can be inspected and questions asked which parents may not feel comfortable doing in the forum of a meeting;
- a more informal activity which aids transition is that of a fun evening for parents and children so that they may visit together and engage in some of the day-to-day activities which happen in Key Stage 1.

The more formal aspects of the Key Stage 1 curriculum also need to be explained to parents and holding workshops on literacy and numeracy are helpful. During these sessions, giving parents advice on how they may help their children at home provides the starting point for the sharing of work in this Key Stage. It is also a time when myths about the requirements of the curriculum at this Key Stage can be dispelled and appropriate ways of working can be discussed, so that parents understand that creativity within the curriculum is still of prime importance and that children still need time to stand and stare.

A team approach to home–school links

Much of what has been discussed in this chapter relies upon a coherent team approach to making home–school links. Practitioners need to share a vision of what parental involvement means and how this is implemented in practice. This can only occur through constant dialogue, reflection and learning through practice. The notion of a two-way communication process is crucial in this respect as practitioners strive to develop ways of working which move easily from setting to home and from home to setting. Whalley (2001: 34) talks about the need for 'a clearly articulated pedagogical approach' that can then be shared with parents. She also discusses the need to employ staff who want to work with parents as well as children, as without the recognition that working with parents is important, then proper involvement will not take place. She states that it 'takes time to establish an equal, active and responsible partnership' (ibid.: 35).

Finally, the more practical elements of involving parents take time. Working as a team and finding time to organise parents' meetings, workshops and open days all have to be negotiated. Even finding time to write reports can be onerous if not properly managed. The importance of teamwork, how this is developed effectively and the practicalities involved will be discussed in the following chapter – Time to work as a team.

CHAPTER 5

Time to work as a team

In the many and varied early years settings there is perhaps one common characteristic: a number of adults work together to meet the needs of children.

(Devereux and Miller 2003: 29)

Organisation, management and leadership

The statement above seems straightforward. However, adults working with young children may not necessarily start with a common view of education and care. Adults will also need guidance on how to work together. These issues provide an important co-ordination challenge. In this chapter we look at the value of spending time on organisation, management and, above all, leadership of teams. In the previous chapters we have considered how to make the best use of time to learn, how to use time to design the curriculum, how time and an effective learning environment are inextricably linked and the importance of taking time to establish partnerships between home and school. These issues contribute to a successful holistic approach to the education and care of young children and cannot be considered in isolation. Time needs to be invested in organisation, management and leadership if the experience for children and adults is to be of high quality. Bringing together hopes and aspirations for high quality provision necessitates organisation and motivation of the team.

Good management also depends on the vision of leadership and the impact that leaders have on their staff team. Rodd (1984: 2) describes leaders as being 'able to balance the concern for work, task, quality and productivity with concern for people, relationships, satisfaction and morale'. This sounds fairly daunting and as Rodd suggests, leadership in early years care and education has traditionally not been considered to be important. She, however, sees the development of leadership skills as a vital challenge, 'if the provision of socially and culturally responsive services for young children and their families is to be successful in the next century' (ibid.: xvii). The implementation of a systematic programme for developing leadership in early years education is outside the remit of this book. Training and development are patchy but there is a growing awareness of the need for professional profiling and career development for early years leaders.

Leadership

Leadership demands interpersonal skills and recognition of the variety of views that members of the team will hold. A true leader is someone who:

- communicates effectively with staff, parents and children;
- influences the way forward through encouraging dialogue and arriving at a team consensus for goals and objectives;
- has drive, enthusiasm and self-confidence and the ability to motivate others;
- is proficient in a wide range of management skills;
- monitors progress and reflects and acts upon failure as well as success;
- is able to care about and relate to individuals, listens to what others have to say and nurtures a team;
- thinks about the future and has a positive attitude to implementing changes and encouraging innovation;
- manages the time needed for adults to help children to establish their confidence and achieve the goals intended for their education and care.

Time taken to consider leadership strategies and the impact they have on the effectiveness of a team is time well spent. Without satisfactory relationships between practitioners there will be a lack of security and trust in the setting and a consequent lack of development and learning for children, parents and staff. Leaders should not be too critical of themselves. They need, however, to be aware of the effect that they have on others and to look for ways of modifying their approach to give practitioners time to explain and discuss. All practitioners need to feel valued in an open and sharing climate where there is good communication.

Communication

Good communication is often taken for granted or left to chance, with little consideration given to effective ways of establishing meaningful dialogue. So very often, despite the best of intentions and years of practice, communications go unheard or are misunderstood, thereby creating barriers to effective team working. Much of this is due to a misunderstanding concerned with the nature of communication. It is not just about conveying information or giving orders to others but is about establishing a true dialogue where ideas are shared. It is also about listening to one another and understanding what is being said. These concepts that underlie true communication will now be discussed further in the following sections.

Establishing dialogue and sharing ideas

The role of the leader is to ensure that the curriculum is planned, 'to take learning forward and to provide opportunities for all children to succeed in an atmosphere of care and of feeling valued' (QCA 2000: 8). In order for these goals to be achieved, the leader has to establish relationships with all team members, including those who may seem peripheral. Each team member needs to feel confident in putting forward ideas and making contributions that will be listened to. In the Reggio Emilia settings in northern Italy the cook is an integral part of the team, with food preparation, nutrition and presentation taken very seriously by staff, parents and children.

Jillian Rodd (1984) stresses the need for early years leaders to have a strong self-image and to be able to demonstrate personal confidence in order to be good communicators. Communication may be achieved through non-verbal signals or body language or it may be outward, verbal and even physical. At all times it should be unambiguous and non-destructive. A leader must attract followers and must be prepared to take time to learn how to communicate. Just as early years practitioners use different ways of communicating with different ages of children, so leaders need to understand the differing needs of team members. Leaders need to understand the values and beliefs of individuals and to be aware of prejudices and anything else that may act as a constraint to communication.

Communication starts with being sensitive to feelings, presenting information and ideas clearly and encouraging contribution from others. Once dialogue has been established, listening and understanding are important aspects of communication to work on.

Listening

Listening to the views of others and understanding what is being said are important elements of communication. Leaders often talk too much when putting forward their viewpoints. Many do not listen to all members of their team. They hear the words but do not take account of what is being said. Listening requires the leader to give:

- time and space for meaningful two-way dialogue;
- time for each person to have their say;
- time to concentrate on the speaker, maintain eye contact, use reassuring gestures and indicate interest;
- time to reflect on what is heard and to take action once the situation has been understood.

Listening requires practice. The natural flow of speech will be interspersed with pauses, time for facial expression and time for contemplation. The advantage of true listening is that the listeners can be more aware of the thought processes of the speakers and have more time for response. There is a more equal partnership between the speaker and the responder when each values the contribution of the other. The strategies used for communication require constant reappraisal. Without a common approach, the members of the team will not feel confident in their ability to share their ideas with children, parents and each other. Nor will they be able to reflect on their own ideas in the light of the views of others. Establishing dialogue and listening to one another provide a framework for good communication. Taking positive action as a result of shared ideas and modified outlook requires time to be spent on team management and on how to be a good member of a team.

How we use time to manage and work as a team

As Devereux and Miller (2003: 30) acknowledge, 'finding time to focus on adult needs can be difficult' but, as we have argued in the introduction to this chapter, it is necessary for practitioners to find the time to communicate with one another in order to provide high quality early years education and care for children and to develop the skills and knowledge of the practitioners who work in the setting.

As in Chapters 3 and 4, in order to address this section on 'how we use time to . . .', we need to ask various questions. First, what do we mean by the team? Is the team made up of everybody who works in the setting or are some team members more equal than others? What underpins effective team working and management? Some teams are highly effective, work well together and have a shared understanding. Other teams are not as effective and engage in a disjointed approach to practice. When do we find time to engage in teamwork and management? Is this something that is ongoing and continually worked at or does it occur at discrete times? Finally, we need to discuss the *how* of teamwork and management. There are many ways that teams work together, but how does time need to be spent in order to make it work? Many of these questions do not have a single and straightforward answer. They depend on the pedagogy, understanding and experience of practitioners. What we can do, however, is draw upon and learn from the practice of effective teams.

Who manages and who is managed?

The concept of the team within early years education and care seems to be a nebulous one in that 'the team' means different things to different people, depending upon the setting in which they work. 'What constitutes a team can vary from centre to centre' (Rodd 1984: 87). Rodd talking about the early years provision in Australia is reassured to find that although the provision is complex, there are similar problems across the continents. In its broadest sense, 'the team' means everyone who works in the setting: teachers, nursery nurses, learning support assistants and other early years practitioners. What about students who visit and work in settings although on a more temporary basis? What is the position of parents? Their work and contribution to children's experiences need to be thought about, planned for and organised, as discussed in Chapter 4. There also needs to be consideration of the work and organisation of other professionals who are not early years educators, for example, speech and language therapists, health visitors and social workers. This aspect of teamwork presents challenges for the leaders of settings and raises interesting issues about the art of delegation and recognition of the skills that each person has to offer. The advent of Children's Centres and Extended Schools, in this country, will provide more opportunities for team working and ways for different professionals to work together.

Each team operates differently depending upon the number of people working in the setting, the complexity of the setting and the way of working of the individual practitioners. All teams will subscribe to some form of hierarchical organisation with due consideration being given to leadership and management. (For a detailed description of leadership and management models, see Lyus 1998: 14–40.) This, however, does not need to be the case.

Within the Reggio Emilia model of early years education, aspects of which have already been described in previous chapters, there is very little hierarchy among teachers and certainly no head teacher. The *pedagogista* acts in an advisory role to a group of four or five settings and holds regular meetings with the team. What also works well is a community-based management system with all stakeholders having a voice, participating in and contributing to the experiences of children within the early years settings. It is seen 'as a means of fostering innovation, protecting educational institutions against the dangers of excessive bureaucracy, and stimulating cooperation between educators and parents' (Spaggiari, in Edwards *et al.* 1998: 99–100). The system is a vital component in ensuring quality experiences for children and their families. Consistent time is invested in this way of working. While this would appear to be a way of working at odds with our current system (Moss, in Abbott and Nutbrown 2001: Chapter 14), the seeds of this approach are being sown through the innovative ways of working and engagement in parent participation demonstrated in the more effective Sure Start programmes currently operating in this country.

As early years educators we need to take time to reflect on these models and consider how we can incorporate a more equal and shared ownership of the team and team working in our own settings.

What is effective team management?

Do we all recognise an effective team and the impact that it has on children's lives? It is difficult to unravel the threads of effective teamwork and management. We have already stated above that a model where all stakeholders are active, participative and equal may offer an effective way forward. There is then greater freedom for dialogue and debate with the opportunity for greater understanding. For this to exist, there needs to be shared understanding of individual roles and responsibilities. Time needs to be given to 'develop ways of working with each other, responding to the needs and idiosyncrasies of colleagues, recognising strengths and weaknesses, and valuing the complementary contributions that each makes to the team effort' (Devereux and Miller 2003: 33). Once this is achieved, teams may speak and act with one voice and when this is the case, it is extremely powerful and reassuring for children, parents and practitioners. This, however, does not negate the continual need for reflection and improvement as discussed later in the chapter.

When do team building and development take place?

As with other aspects of early years education, discussed in previous chapters, discussion and resolution need to be ongoing. 'Valuable staff time needs to be used effectively' (ibid.: 31). In teams that work happily and effectively, dialogue, debate, thinking, reflection and reassessment occur as a part of everyday life. It must be noted that when teams first work together this will not necessarily be the case and as team members change, there will need to be negotiation and readjustment. It is important for team members to discuss their work informally and also to have a clear structure for regular group meetings.

Daily meetings
It is important to 'designate a daily, uninterrupted time for the team to meet' (Hohman and Weikart 1995: 92). This is necessary so that:

- team members can share observations and assessment of children and plan for their progress accordingly;
- time is allowed to discuss the environment and make changes depending on individual and group needs;
- adjustments can be made to the curriculum in response to children's needs;
- there can be communication with parents so they are kept informed of their children's needs and experiences and are able to share their thoughts with staff.

The daily meeting may not include all members of the team at the same time. Within the Foundation Stage it may be that reception staff meet separately from nursery staff, individual class teams meet together or that group teams meet together. What is of paramount importance is that key team members meet together daily.

Weekly meetings
Teams also need to meet together on a weekly basis and at this time the focus for the meeting will be different from the focus during a daily meeting. It will be necessary at these meetings:

- for the whole Foundation Stage team to meet together in order to ensure continuity and cohesion across the age phase;
- to organise planning for the next week and into the longer term;
- for the whole team to consider the weekly timetable and changes that need to be made in the light of recent experiences and forthcoming events.

Monthly meetings

Monthly meetings are needed in order to discuss pedagogy. There will be ongoing discussion of practice; questioning what is done and why and consideration of the way forward. All these smaller conversations need to be pulled together. In effective teams, monthly meetings provide a chance to:

- share thoughts, reflections and concerns of the team;
- debate changes to practice;
- plan for longer joint sessions for writing, explanation and implementation of policy documents;
- allow practitioners to grow and develop in their understanding and to be confident in putting forward views and responding.

Finally, time needs to be given to team meetings that may be intermittent and sometimes spontaneous. They will be organised to respond to the continuing or particular needs of the setting. They might include:

- planning and organising special events and open days and looking at the role of practitioners, parents and other team members;
- planning and organising workshops for parents;
- evaluating and re-writing policy documents. Much of the thinking for these will arise out of the monthly pedagogy meetings but time needs to be found for joint writing and implementation of policy documents;
- taking time on a regular basis to develop a culture of self-evaluation and research.

Overall, teamwork needs patience in 'establishing an honest dialogue about specific curriculum issues, levelling with people, getting to know team members in a more than superficial way, learning from one another's strengths and differences – all these processes take time' (Hohman and Weikart 1995: 95).

How to ensure effective team working

In this section we look at ways of working that enable teams to achieve the 'what' of effective team working. In the above section we have identified reasons why different types of meetings occur at different times. For meetings to be effective people need to communicate (this aspect of effective team working has been discussed earlier in the chapter). Through clear communication individual roles and responsibilities should be understood.

Job descriptions provide a starting point for understanding roles and responsibilities. Much of the work in early years settings is informal and job descriptions are hard to recognise. Early years practitioners need to discuss and agree the nature of their jobs, both informal and formal. Negotiation may be necessary, where roles and responsibilities overlap and where there is an opportunity for sharing responsibility to ensure greater understanding of children's development.

Observation of practice

As well as articulating and understanding roles and responsibilities, another way of gaining insight and facilitating effective team working is observation of one another. This may strike fear into the hearts of many practitioners but when handled sensitively it is a powerful way of working. A format for observing colleagues' ways of working is provided within the guidance for the Effective Early Learning Project (Pascal *et al.* 1996). The Adult Engagement Schedule requires adults to be observed across three categories: sensitivity, stimulation and autonomy. Sensitivity is concerned with how sensitive an adult is to the feelings and well-being of children; stimulation refers to how well an adult stimulates children; and autonomy is the amount of freedom an adult gives children to experiment. When using the schedule there is the opportunity to rate adults' performance in these categories but this formality is not necessary for gaining insight and understanding of another person's practice. Observing and discussing observations enables adults to share in each other's strengths and weaknesses and as a consequence strengthen their own practice and improve team working.

Teams can also be drawn together through engaging in joint activities, which contribute to team development. Through discussion of objectives for the team to work on and by participating in joint training, through in-service days and attending conferences, a shared vision and understanding should develop across the team. As this occurs, teams will work more cohesively with one another.

Finally, in this section there needs to be some consideration of the practicalities involved in enabling meetings to occur, observations to be undertaken and training events to be attended. Time needs to be negotiated and systems put in place to ensure that while meeting adults' needs, children's needs are still paramount. This may be through the creative deployment of staff, the use of rotas and timetables, keeping time logs, making and keeping to agendas for meetings and other time management techniques that work for individual teams.

The setting in which practitioners work will also influence team working and the ability to organise and participate in meetings. For those practitioners working in playgroups, for example, there is potentially a pressure on the amount of time that the accommodation is available. Time will have to be spent on getting equipment out and putting it away and this will reduce the amount of time for practitioners to meet. For practitioners who work within a Foundation Stage setting in a primary school, there will be the additional pressure of the need to attend whole school meetings. A member of the Foundation Stage team should be a member of the Senior Management Team and will then have those meetings to attend as well. These additional demands will have to be negotiated in order that practitioners do not spend too great a proportion of their time in meetings to the detriment of their work with children.

There are also other, more fundamental problems to overcome. As discussed in Chapter 1, there are many factors which influence philosophy or what we believe in and pedagogy, how we think it should be done. This will also impact on team working and may include:

- experience – practitioners may not have experience of effective team working and may need to be convinced of the need to work in this way;

- training – practitioners may not have received input on team working as a part of their training and again may need to be convinced of its merits.

Once these problems have been recognised and discussion is helping practitioners to come to a common understanding of the ethos of the setting, effective team working should follow. Once established, it needs to be maintained and this is the subject of the next section.

Sustaining and developing teamwork

Rodd (1984: 88) describes a team as 'a group of people cooperating with each other to work towards an agreed set of aims, objectives or goals while simultaneously considering the personal needs and interests of individuals'.

In the first section of this chapter we discussed the importance of clear communication for the benefit of the team and for the benefit of the children in the setting. The second section considered the composition of teams and the *who, what, when* and *how* of effective team working. In this final section we explore how teamwork can be sustained and developed.

Undoubtedly teamwork plays an important part in early education. The findings from unpublished research (Rodd 1984: 88) identified advantages, including: acknowledgement of professionalism and a sense of belonging, opportunities to address problems and reduce conflict, opportunities for responsibility and leadership, the chance to share ideas, resources and tasks while working towards common goals.

As has been discussed earlier, the successful team leader is one who is a skilled manager, communicates clearly, listens, motivates, develops self-esteem, is able to delegate and looks upon change as a positive challenge. Successful teamwork should allow each member to contribute expertise, resources and enthusiasm. The climate should be one of co-operation and shared decision-making. The reality, however, is that the leader has to take responsibility, particularly when things go wrong.

In the Reggio Emilia approach to early education, in northern Italy, the particular culture of the teams is well documented. Knight (in Abbott and Nutbrown 2001: 32) sees the interaction of parents, children, staff and the wider community as being at the heart of the Reggio philosophy. She describes the team as 'the professional community'. This community undertakes genuine dialogue, raising and answering questions about children's thinking and learning. The community encourages presentation and discussion of conflicting and controversial views to help gain new insight. The community or team is confident to discuss the processes of learning as well as the outcomes and is able to involve parents fully in the organisation of their children's education. There is a strong intellectual flavour to the discussions and an eagerness to refer to research and past experience. Ideas are shared between settings both immediately with the help of the *pedagogista* and through the amazing *documentation* of children's work archived and available for study in a central record centre. The *pedagogista* is a senior practitioner who provides an internal and an external role. She has responsibility for a small group of settings, which she visits once a week. Her internal role enables her to build a relationship with staff, children and parents. In the setting she is able to focus on the documented evidence of children's learning and offer theoretical and practical advice and inspiration. Outside the setting her role is in encouraging collaboration between settings and providing a link between the community, the municipality, and the wider Italian and international communities. She provides the *team* with the chance to reflect, question and solve problems.

This style of leadership works very well for the Reggio settings. As a visitor, one is struck by the professionalism of all the staff, their eagerness to discuss their philosophy and their astonishing knowledge of the potential of each child. This very high level of adult self-esteem, collaboration with each other and willingness to share their expertise is only achieved through a consistent allocation of time. Table 5.1 is adapted from Knight (in Abbott and Nutbrown 2001: 32) and shows the hours needed to develop and maintain this style of teamwork.

Table 5.1 Time allocation for teamwork

Teachers	Hours per year
Time outside the classroom	190 – of which
In-service training	107
Working with parents	43
Discussion of projects and documentation of work	40

Probably the most important observations made when experiencing this way of working are:

- the extremely high levels of job satisfaction;
- the way that the time allocated for in-depth discussion and the variety of training increase knowledge and integrity and provide a firm foundation for staff to be responsible and innovative practitioners;
- the willingness and confidence that all staff have in explaining their ideals and showing how they interact with children.

Although many visitors experience a language barrier, it is apparent that the same willingness and confidence are present in the children, who spend time in communicating ideas through physical demonstration, gesture and graphic representation.

We can learn a great deal about team working from this model although we are mostly working in a system where the leader maintains a constant presence. Our teams are also often unnecessarily small, particularly where the opportunity for a Foundation Stage Team in an infant school has not been fully explored. The advantages of our system are that there can be continuous monitoring and possible immediate conflict resolution as well as celebration of success. The disadvantages are that the team may feel inhibited and over-scrutinised. This in turn leads to the team taking less initiative and fewer risks. Whatever the system in place, there are important characteristics that develop within a team and help to sustain its effectiveness. There should be a chance for:

- constructive and open communication;
- sharing of the short-term and long-term goals;
- sharing knowledge, understanding and observation of children's development;
- mutual respect and support and recognition of each other's skills;
- co-operation, commitment and motivation;
- confidence in talking to parents, other staff and visitors;
- awareness of the collective views on education while at the same time having the opportunity to be flexible and innovative;
- sharing and celebrating success and reflecting on and repairing failure.

Maintenance and development of teams are complex tasks. The leader plays an important role but it is the contribution from each team member and skilful deployment of responsibility that will make or break a team. Jillian Rodd (1994) clearly describes very realistic stages of team development. The following list has been adapted from her work:

- A leader 'needs to provide clear direction and guidelines for staff . . . which will communicate her vision and values' (Rodd 1984: 93). This will include existing team members and the integration of new staff.

- The team members need to feel comfortable with one another. As well as professional meetings, social get togethers may help to cement relationships.

- Conflict will inevitably arise as team members grow in confidence and begin to challenge the leadership and negotiate for roles and responsibilities. The leader has to recognise that this is a normal part of group identity but, if left unchecked, will destroy the vision for the setting. The leader will need to adopt professional strategies to help resolve differences between staff. The small group and larger meetings discussed in the previous section should help to clarify expectations, provide opportunities to talk through problems and establish new goals.

- It is useful for staff to have personal goals with a chance to follow up through either formal or informal review.

- Once consensus and co-operation have been achieved, then meetings that consider innovation, research and modification of practice can take place. Confidence will have been gained through resolution of conflicts and what Rodd (ibid.) describes as 'risk taking' will be possible.

- Morale needs to be maintaincd. Team members need to become involved in setting goals, writing policies and ensuring that they can be implemented. As discussed in the previous section, meetings will be held to establish the ground rules and smaller working groups can take responsibility for specific areas.

- As confidence in accepting challenges increases, then information needs to be shared, consensual decisions arrived at and there needs to be willingness to take risks and bring about change.

- As development takes place, enthusiasm and motivation should follow. Rodd (ibid.: 96) talks about 'previously inactive members of staff' becoming 'more involved with a broader range of responsibilities in the centre'.

- The leader needs to be vigilant! As the potential of the team evolves, there needs to be reassurance and encouragement. The focus needs to be on relationships and sharing of expertise. The atmosphere must be one where there is a serious purpose and vision for the children's experience in the setting as well as one where there is fun and laughter.

- Disagreements and conflicts should be short-lived and they should be handled sensitively and quickly to maintain the consensus and co-operation that have been achieved.

- The involvement of staff in setting goals, good communication, acknowledgement of success and constructive review will strengthen the resolve of the team and ensure that there is pride in the goals that are being achieved.

- Once an effective team has been established, the members will enjoy their work and will be happy that the contribution they make is a part of the overall effectiveness of the setting.

- The leader cannot sit back! Continual reflection, slight adjustments, introduction to new groups and ideas, taking opportunities to share expertise outside the setting all form a part of staff development. Time needs to be taken to identify and address individual needs and to encourage team members to share newly found knowledge.

Rodd (ibid.) identifies an inevitable change in the cohesion and common purpose of a team. When a leader is replaced or there is another significant change in a team there must be a period of *mourning*. There has to be a period of time when regrouping and reordering are essential. Previous success must be celebrated and time taken to adapt to change and to find a framework for the way forward.

In this and the previous chapters we have looked at time and different aspects of early years education and practice. Throughout the discussion we have asked questions about time and how this important aspect of all our lives may be utilised best for the benefit of all children with whom we work. Hopefully the ideas have also provoked dialogue between practitioners in early years settings and generated informal questioning of practice. The following chapter – Time to self-evaluate – provides a more formal framework, which practitioners in early years teams may utilise to self-evaluate their use of time with young children.

CHAPTER 6

Time to self-evaluate

Research may constitute 'illuminative evaluation' where researchers seek to combine evaluation with professional development in order to improve the quality of early childhood education through the consideration of the processes of learning as well as setting and context.

(Aubrey *et al.* 2000: 86)

Now is the time to focus on evaluation. The previous chapters have looked at understanding and using time across different areas of early years practice. This chapter provides an opportunity for practitioners to reflect on their own understanding, beliefs and practice in relation to time and presents a guide to self-evaluation of how time is used and practice, which should have an impact upon children's experiences.

Evaluation

Evaluation is not a new concept in early years practice. Pascal *et al.* (1996) presented an exemplar guide to evaluation through the Effective Early Learning project. Recently there has been the evaluation of early excellence centres (Ofsted 2004b) and currently there is the national evaluation of the Sure Start programmes which can be accessed at www.ness.bbk.ac.uk. Evaluation builds on the concept of teachers as reflective practitioners and as researchers which is embedded within the Reggio Emilia approach to early years education: 'To learn and relearn together with the children is our line of work . . . Our teachers do research either on their own or with their colleagues to produce strategies that favour children's work or can be utilized by them' (Edwards *et al.* 1998: 86).

So what is evaluation? 'Evaluation is a process which helps us see more clearly what it is we are doing, and the nature of the issues being confronted. It is a way of seeing' (adapted from Downie and McNeish 2000: 1.1). This definition firmly shows evaluation to be an ongoing process, which enables us to understand what we do, why we do it and the potential impact we can have. One of the underpinning principles of evaluation is that it should be a part of learning and a way of sharing successes and difficulties. Pascal and Bertram further exemplify this and state that evaluation is concerned with improving quality of provision and that there are some common ground rules, which inform evaluative work. Some of these are that:

- there need to be judgements made about quality;
- there should be open, honest and collaborative dialogue for evaluation to be effective;
- extended time is needed for dialogue;
- there needs to be a framework in which evaluation can take place;
- the evidence from evaluation should be shared with all concerned;
- evaluation should result in action planning.

(adapted from Pascal and Bertram 1997: 9)

As is evident from the above, evaluation takes time but must be a part of ongoing practice. The findings from evaluation should be used to make the process worthwhile and ultimately bring benefit to children, parents and practitioners. The process of evaluation should enable us to identify our current position – where are we now? It should also help us clarify where we want to be and what will be different once we have got there. In our evaluation of time and how we use it in our practice in early years settings we should go some way towards answering the question: *How can we use time more effectively to benefit our practice and the experiences that we offer to the children we work with?*

It must be remembered that this process is dynamic. We will never arrive at ultimate best practice and we should always be open to critical appraisal of new ideas and examples of practice and be prepared to adapt and modify them to further improve our work with young children.

How to use the self-evaluation frameworks

In order to complete work on self-evaluation, time needs to be found for the team to reflect on their practice. The frameworks that follow include questions that are intended to stimulate discussion between the team members. Tables 6.1–6.5 present five frameworks for evaluation, each based on the topic discussed in Chapters 1–5 of this book. There must be an ethos within the team that allows people to speak openly and honestly. People need to be heard and listened to without facing hostility. This is not to say that there will not be disagreement. Consensus will only be arrived at if all angles are explored in an atmosphere where everyone is entitled to express their opinions and to feel that their contribution is worth while (see Chapter 5).

From a discussion that is based on practitioners' beliefs, knowledge and experience, evidence should be provided, which will enable all practitioners to understand what informs their practice and where they are at any point in time. Discussions should provide evidence to celebrate the successes of practice. There will also need to be evidence that challenges the effectiveness of other areas of practice and suggests the need for change. As Edwards *et al.* (1998: 86) say, 'When all the teachers in the school are in agreement, the projects, strategies, and styles of work become intertwined and the school becomes a truly different school.'

You may not find it necessary to complete every aspect of this self-evaluation. It is organised under the themes for each chapter (Tables 6.1–6.5). This allows you to focus on areas of practice that are particularly pertinent to you at the present time and that fit into the development plan for your setting. We would suggest, however, that all teams undertake the self-evaluation for Chapter 1 as this will provide a starting point in terms of identifying the theoretical and pedagogical understanding of the team.

All the questions within the evaluation frameworks can be used to form the basis of a series of staff meetings and will enable the team to reflect on and audit their skills, beliefs and practice concerning their work with young children. We would also recommend that prior to embarking on each section it would be helpful to reread the relevant chapter first. This will provide the team with an overview of the issues to be discussed.

Evaluation and Chapter 1 – How do we recognise and value time with children?

You now have an opportunity to discuss and reflect on your practice in relation to the issues raised in this chapter. At the end of this section it should be possible to write your own statement about how you recognise and use time with the children in your setting. It will also provide the starting point for auditing the other issues related to time that are outlined in this book.

As stated in Chapter 1, there are many factors which impact on our understanding and use of time with young children. The questions in Table 6.1 address the different areas outlined in the chapter and relate to the experiences of all the team members. They are intended to provide a stimulus for whole-team discussion and enable understanding of practice. Some questions are quite broad and are concerned with experiences and understanding while others are more specific and are related to knowledge and practice. Exemplars are provided as a guide only. For this framework to be useful and to have a positive impact on practice with children, the questions must be answered honestly and openly.

When you have evaluated your understanding and practice against the issues raised in Chapter 1 you should be in a position to analyse your findings and write a statement for visitors to your setting outlining how you recognise and value time with children. This statement should include a brief discussion of why the team feel time is important for young children. It should detail why and

Table 6.1 Questions for evaluation: How do we recognise and value time with children?

Question	Exemplar	Evidence
Type of setting		
What settings have each of the team members worked in?	• playgroup • nursery class in a primary school	
How was time organised in these settings?	• quiet time and activity time • a timetable with different activities every half hour	
What was the practice in these settings?	• organised with time for children to follow their own activities and time for adult-initiated activities • lots of adult-led activities	
Pedagogy		
What do team members understand by the term 'pedagogy'?	• practice • relating theory to practice	
Training		
What qualifications do team members have?	• Level 3 in Early Years • B.Ed. in Education	
What do team members understand about child development?	• all the areas of development • PILESS (Bruce and Meggitt 2002)	
What do team members understand about early years care and education?		
Children learning		
How are children given opportunities to be active?	• access to the outside area • physical activities inside	
How are children given opportunities to use language?	• talk to adults • talk to children	
How are children given opportunities to work with others?	• work in small groups • work in a large group	
How are children helped to feel secure?	• by bringing in toys from home	
How are children helped to experience success?	• by observing them and supporting their learning	
Theory		
Which early years pioneers and theories of learning are team members familiar with?	• Montessori-trained • Studied early years pioneers as part of early childhood degree	
How has this informed practice in the setting?	• types of resources • using observation to inform practice	

how time is organised to facilitate children's learning. There should also be an explanation of how children learn and how time is used to maximise children's opportunities for learning.

Evaluation and Chapter 2 – Time to learn

In Chapter 2 we put forward the argument that learning takes time. This is an argument which is clearly supported by *The Curriculum Guidance for the Foundation Stage* (QCA 2000). We looked at principles that underpin how we use time to create and implement an effective curriculum for children. We also discussed how to organise time to create a stimulating environment. The discussion involved looking at timetabling, space, resources and display. Table 6.2 presents questions which should provide you with evidence to evaluate your use of time in terms of curriculum design and use of the environment.

Table 6.2 Questions for evaluation: Time to learn

Question	Evidence

Implementing the curriculum framework in your setting
How much time is spent on the curriculum in the:
  long term?
  medium term?
  short term?	

What opportunities are there to make cross-curricular links and to allow for holistic learning?	
How are children enabled to have time to engage in in-depth learning?	
How are children enabled to have time to make their own links in their learning?	
How much time is spent on adult-directed activities?	
How much time is spent on child-initiated activities?	
How is time made for adults and children to engage in sustained shared thinking?	
The daily timetable How much time is spent on children being active?	
How much time is spent on children being sedentary?	

How much time is spent in:
    whole-class activities?
    small group activities?
    one-to-one activities?

The environment: physical space
How is the space organised?
How much time is spent outside?
How much time is spent inside?

The environment: resources
What resources are available?
How are resources organised?
How do children access resources?

The environment: displays
What do the team feel is the purpose
of display?
How much time is spent on display?
Who organises displays?
What is displayed?

Now that you have completed this section, you should be able to use the evidence to start to inform further discussion and perhaps change your practice in this area. Through this discussion there may be a shared understanding of what is meant by the curriculum which may lead to changes in how the curriculum for children is organised over time or how cross-curricular links are made more visible.

There may be a reorganisation of time so that less time is spent on adult-directed activities and more on child-initiated activities. Alongside this there may be a discussion of the adult's role during child-initiated activities. This again may lead to change. Or a reappraisal of the daily timetable or elements of it so that the proportion of time spent between active and sedentary activities is altered. Also within this section there is an opportunity to evaluate the use of the environment and this may lead to changes being made to the space, resources or displays.

Evaluation and Chapter 3 – Time to assess

In this chapter we put forward the argument that assessment should be an integral part of teaching and learning and looked at the need for informal and formal assessment. We also discussed how we use time to look at and listen to children. The discussion involved identifying a range of practical strategies for assessing children and how time should be used to ensure that this is a part of everyday practice.

Now that you have completed this section, you should be able to use the evidence to start to inform further discussion and maybe change your practice in this area.

Table 6.3   Questions for evaluation: Time to assess

Question	Evidence
Who assesses? How do parents contribute to the assessment process?	
How do all adults in the setting contribute to the assessment process?	
How do other practitioners contribute to the assessment process?	
How does the child contribute to the assessment process?	
What is assessed? How are children's attitudes to learning assessed?	
How are children's interests assessed?	
How are the different learning areas of the curriculum framework assessed? • personal, social and emotional development • language and literacy • mathematical development • knowledge and understanding of the world • physical development • creative development	
When does assessment take place? How frequently does assessment occur?	
When are planned assessments conducted?	
When are spontaneous assessments conducted?	
How do you assess? What methods are used to listen to children?	
What methods are used to talk to children?	
What methods are used to observe children?	
How do you use the information gained from the various assessments?	
Sharing assessment information How are assessments organised and shared?	

When do you share assessment information with:
    parents?
    children?
    each other?
    other professionals?	

How is assessment information used to inform report writing and the Foundation Stage Profile?	

Discussion may result in shared understanding concerning assessment. Again, it is likely that you will see the need to make some changes. Identifying who is involved in the assessment process may lead to greater involvement by some parties, for example, parents. Evaluation may uncover discrepancies in what is being evaluated and whether a greater proportion of assessment time is spent on some curriculum areas to the detriment of others. There may then be an opportunity to work out a better balance.

After this very important evaluation exercise a change in assessment methods may be appropriate. The 'tools' used in the assessment process may be diversified, allowing for greater variety and depth of assessment. Examples are given in the discussion of documentation. Finally, there may be a change in how assessments are shared, with whom they are shared and how information from assessment is used in report writing and any transfer of information about young children.

Evaluation and Chapter 4 – Time to develop a home–school partnership

In this chapter we asked whether we understand and value the child's world at home and use this knowledge to make an effective home–school partnership. This can be hotly discussed and debated and is often a confused and confusing issue for practitioners. In order to aid this process we have made a distinction between involving parents and being in partnership with parents. To be of maximum benefit to children, however, we argue that time needs to be made to engage parents in a true partnership. We have adapted the model from Whalley (2001) to provide a starting point for reflective thinking in this area of early years care and education.

Table 6.4 Questions for evaluation: Time to develop a home–school partnership

Question	Evidence
Who makes home–school links? How are practitioners involved in making links with parents and carers?	
How does the team share information from making links with parents and carers?	
What links do we make between home and school? How does information about a child's background and culture influence practice in the setting?	
How does information about a child's interests, likes and dislikes influence the attitudes and interactions in the setting?	

How does information about a child's development influence the way in which we work?

How is information about a child's local community reflected in the provision within the setting?

How do we make home–school links?
  Initial visits
How is knowledge gained about children before they enter the setting?
How is this information used to make transition easier?

  Nurturing home–school links
How are items and information from home valued in the setting?

How are written links made between home and school?

How are activities built into the curriculum which value home experiences?

Sustaining and developing home–school links
What open days and workshops are organised for parents and carers?

How are parents' and carers' interests and skills incorporated into children's experiences in the setting?

How is the local community able to contribute to children's experiences in the setting?

How are parents and carers encouraged to sustain educational practice in the home?

What processes are in place to reach parents and carers who are difficult to engage?

What processes are in place to ease transition from the Foundation Stage to Key Stage 1?

Now that you have completed this section you should be able to use the evidence to start to inform further discussion and maybe change your practice in this area. There could be changes in how home–school links are made. There may be more activities for parents to help them either to understand what their children are doing in the setting, or to give them the opportunity to work at their own level to understand more about what the children are learning. There may be an exploration of and greater links with the local community. Finally, there may be increased dialogue and work with Key Stage 1 colleagues in order to aid children's transition from the Foundation Stage.

Evaluation and Chapter 5 – Time to work as a team

In this chapter we have argued for the value of spending time on organisation, management and, most importantly, leadership in order to ensure there is high quality provision for both children and parents. We have defined what we mean by leadership and discussed how this is an evolving concept affected particularly by the rapid changes in early years education. We have also discussed the difficulties in providing effective leadership. We looked at the importance of effective communication in building up a team. The team needs a shared vision for early education. The team needs to work together to improve the experiences for children in early years settings. The following questions will enable teams to evaluate their practice in this area.

Table 6.5 Questions for evaluation: Time to work as a team

Question	Evidence
How are team members enabled to understand their own and each other's job descriptions?	
How is time managed to ensure that one-to-one meetings take place?	
How are issues raised from these meetings used to inform practice?	
How is time managed for daily meetings to take place?	
How are issues raised from these meetings used to inform practice?	
How is time managed for weekly meetings to take place?	
How are issues raised from these meetings used to inform practice?	
How is time managed for monthly meetings to take place?	
How are issues raised from these meetings used to inform practice?	
How is time managed to enable practitioners to observe one another?	
How is information from these observations shared and used to inform practice?	
How is time managed so that practitioners may engage in joint activities which develop their practice?	

Now that you have completed this section you should be able to use the evidence to start to inform further discussion and perhaps change your practice in this area. Evaluation of this area should enable the team to have greater understanding of each other's roles and how they may contribute effectively to the team. There may be more focused team meetings that can lead to changes in practice. Or sensitive discussions regarding peer observation that can lead to changes in attitude and more confidence in being watched and in evaluating what has been observed. Finally, there may be opportunities for individual practitioners to develop their own expertise in areas which have interested them during this evaluation.

Evaluation summary

Now that this process of evaluation has been completed you are in a position to bring all your findings together and formulate an action plan for future development. In order to analyse your findings all team members need to:

- celebrate the team's successes;
- identify the team's weaknesses;
- prioritise the areas for development.

The areas identified for development will be the framework for an action plan. Once this has been arrived at, you will need to identify the resources and support you will need to facilitate work on the first stages of the action plan. This may involve:

- further training for staff members;
- setting aside time during an in-service day to work as a team;
- using the expertise of an external consultant;
- buying additional resources to facilitate children's learning and development;
- making organisational changes to either the environment, support structures, planning and assessment mechanisms or staff;
- identifying different ways of working with, for example, parents and the local community.

Finally, you will need to draw up a timetable for change and allocate responsibility to staff for different aspects of the action plan. You will also need to allocate time to review the changes and the impact they are having on roles, responsibilities and practice of the staff and the experiences that children are receiving. You may wish to return to relevant questions from this evaluation framework to help you with these review sessions. Obviously this process of evaluation is a cyclical one and continuing reflection on your practice in this area will result in more effective use of time with the children in your setting.

Evaluation of practice and implementation of change constitute a dynamic process. It is exciting to see things improve and is important for the self-confidence of practitioners to be able to articulate the aims and objectives of the setting and to watch children flourish in an environment where time to learn is respected. Don't allow complacency to set in. Be constantly aware of the need to question and reflect. How we use time with children will affect their view of the world and will affect the type of citizens they will become.

Conclusion

What is this life if, full of care,
We have no time to stand and stare.

(W.H. Davies)

We used W.H. Davies's poem as an introduction to our discussion of using time in early years education. It was a poem that we both remembered from our childhood and one that seemed to support our belief that many children have little, or no, opportunity to 'stand and stare' during their time in the Foundation Stage. In addition, those adults working in the Foundation Stage also have little, or no, opportunity to 'stand and stare'. Children and adults are often rushed from one activity to the next. In the introduction we discussed the ever-increasing pace of life. This affects not just children's experiences in school, but all our experiences on a daily basis. This means that the opportunity to reflect and muse on problems and savour experiences is lost. Overall, it means that children are given very little time to think. As Pound says

> The wide range of contemporary pressures placed on young children and their families mean that children need time and space to deal with their anxieties. They need time and space to take some risks – not an easy thing to do when you feel insecure. Above all they need time and space to think. Taking time to think, Claxton (1998) reminds us, does not always involve more time – it simply demands unpressured time.
>
> (in Fisher 2002b: 24)

We hope we have argued persuasively for the need for unpressured time and for a reorganisation or reallocation of time when working with young children and how children and adults may benefit from this.

Each chapter has focused on different aspects of early years education and how time might be organised and managed to ensure effective practice in these areas. A constant theme running throughout the chapters has been the example of the Reggio Emilia approach to early years education. In this educational experience learning is promoted through a shared understanding of the child and their world. Adults and children work together using a rhythm and pace suited to deep thinking and astonishing problem solving. The adult and the child each have time for the other. The key messages from each chapter are highlighted in the conclusion with a brief summary of the use of time within the Reggio Emilia approach.

Key messages from Chapter 1 – How do we recognise and value time with children?

- *Use of time in the Foundation Stage is highly variable.* This varies according to many different factors including type of setting, beliefs of practitioners and the age of the children in the setting.

- *Children in the Foundation Stage spend too much time engaged in sedentary activities.* An example was given of a timetable from a Foundation Stage setting. However, this is not an isolated example. Our work with students over many years has shown us that this is the case in many settings. Of course, we have also been privileged to visit many Foundation Stage settings where children are active and engaged in purposeful learning.

- *Children can be in educational settings from three years of age and, therefore, their time needs to be used so that it is appropriate to their age and stage of development.* This means that practitioners must have an understanding of child development and how children learn.

- *Practitioners' use of time with young children has been influenced by many different factors and experiences.* This has been exemplified in the chapter. The evaluation framework for this chapter enables practitioners to explore these influences and reflect upon how they have informed their practice.

- *Practitioners may have worked in different settings, which use time in different ways.* Again, the variety of settings which practitioners may have worked in have been described in the chapter. It is important for practitioners to recognise the influence that working in different settings will have had on their practice and to build upon these experiences.

- *Practitioners will have received a variety of training, which will impact on how they use time.* Practitioners need to reflect on this, identify gaps in skills and/or knowledge and perhaps engage in further training.

- *Practitioners may hold different views of children and childhood, which influence their use of time.* How views of children and childhood impact on teaching is an under-researched area of early years education. However, it is one that needs careful consideration and further investigation.

- *Practitioners' use of time may be influenced by the age of the child with whom they work.* As already stated, it is important that practitioners have an understanding of how children develop and learn in order to interact with them appropriately.

- *Practitioners need to understand how children learn in order to use time appropriately with them.* Once practitioners are aware of the elements involved in how children learn they can provide an environment, curriculum and interactions that support their learning.

- *Practitioners need to engage in ongoing training to ensure that they have a clear understanding of children and practice which can help them to use time effectively.* Further training needs to be focused on early years practice and complement and build upon previous training.

- *Different educational theories influence practitioners' use of time.* These theories have been discussed in the chapter and have subtle but important influences on the use of time with young children.

- *Different philosophical and educational frameworks influence practitioners' use of time.* Again, the evaluation framework enables practitioners to explore these influences on their practice and use of time with children.

Key messages from Chapter 2 – Time to learn

- *Learning takes time.* As stated in the introduction, everyone needs time to reflect and think. To think in depth and problem solve is fundamental learning.

- *Time is embedded within the Curriculum Guidance for the Foundation Stage, both within the principles and within the areas of learning.* Within this chapter, time within the Curriculum Guidance was highlighted and exemplified with underpinning quotes.

- *Planning in the long, medium and short term requires creative and careful consideration.* Planning takes time and needs to be considered over different time scales. Various examples of planning from different Foundation Stage settings were given to show how planning could be creative and appropriate.

- *The use of 'the hour' in the Literacy and Numeracy Strategies should be broken down in order to be implemented effectively and appropriately for young children.* 'The hour' within Foundation Stage settings has been debated in the early years literature. Despite official guidance stating that a full hour did not need to be in place until the end of the reception year, it was often in place during the autumn term. An example of effective implementation was given in the chapter.

- *Practitioners must analyse the balance of time between active and sedentary activities in the daily timetable.* All timetables should be scrutinised as exemplified in the chapter. Where necessary, alterations should be made to ensure that children receive a balance of active and sedentary activities appropriate to their age and stage of development.

- *Practitioners must ensure that time is spent in all areas of the setting.* In addition to this, how the space is organised and used should also be reviewed.

- *Children should be given time to explore and use resources thoughtfully.* A range of resources should be provided that engage children and promote learning.

Key messages from Chapter 3 – Time to assess

- *Assessment takes time.* Gathering a range of information on young children that informs planning, provision and record keeping is time-consuming.

- *Time needs to be organised so that all people can contribute to the assessment process.* Finding out about young children requires information to be gathered from a variety of sources. This takes time but is necessary if a true picture of a child is to be developed.

- *All aspects of a child's development need to be assessed.* Again, this takes time. Time is needed to observe and assess all areas of development. It is also necessary to take time to understand and make sense of the information.

- *All factors which contribute to a child's experience in the Foundation Stage need to be assessed: the environment and those who work with the child.* Assessment is not only about gathering information about a child, it also involves assessing how a child uses the environment, and how they work and interact with others.

- *Time needs to be organised for planned as well as spontaneous assessments.* There needs to be a balance between both types of assessment, as this will generate different information.

- *Assessment involves looking at and listening to the child and a range of assessment techniques need to be employed.* The evaluation framework for this chapter enables practitioners to reflect on the assessment techniques they use and to identify areas for improvement.

- *All adults involved with the child need to have time to engage in dialogue about the child.* In order to have a complete understanding of the child, all those who work with the child need to share information.

- *The Foundation Stage Profile is not enough – other forms of assessment must be used and a 'learning journey' of a child's time in the Foundation Stage kept.* While an important document, the Foundation Stage Profile must be informed by, and supplemented by, other forms of assessment. Compiling all this information and reflecting upon it enable a learning journey to be kept of a child's time in the Foundation Stage.

Key messages from Chapter 4 – Time to develop a home–school partnership

- *Time must be invested in developing a partnership with parents.* If an effective partnership with parents is to be built up, time must be invested in the process.

- *Developing a partnership with parents requires the participation of all those who work with the child.* A partnership is not just between one practitioner and the parent but between all those who work in the setting and the child and the family.

- *Time must be taken to understand the child's world outside of the early years setting.* In order to develop a true partnership, practitioners need to understand the child's world. Time needs to be given to develop this knowledge and understanding.

- *Understanding the child's world begins before the child enters the Foundation Stage.* In addition to the above, time must be taken to understand the other settings the child has been in prior to the Foundation Stage.

- *Nurturing home–school links necessitates time for talking, observing and sharing.* There needs to be time for practitioners to talk to each other and time for practitioners to talk and share with parents.

- *Sustaining home–school links is a two-way process and communication is central to this.* Parents need to know that they are welcome in the setting and have as much right to ask questions about their child in the setting as practitioners do about the child in the home. Information about a child's life should be shared between setting and home in different ways.

- *Time needs to be found to reach parents who are difficult to engage in this process.* This is an area of practice that needs creative ways of working to reach these families.

- *Time needs to be invested in ensuring that the transition from the Foundation Stage to Key Stage 1 is smooth for everyone involved.* Working with Key Stage 1 colleagues to ensure this happens successfully is time-consuming.

- *Time needs to be invested in team working to ensure a successful home–school partnership.* None of this will work unless the team work together and have a shared understanding and vision of what is meant by a home–school partnership.

Key messages from Chapter 5 – Time to work as a team

- *Leadership is integral to effective team working and this takes time to be developed.* Leadership in early years education had not been prioritised in the past. However, time must be spent on it and it must be prioritised to ensure that teams work effectively in any setting.

- *Time is necessary for teams to communicate.* Communication is crucial to effective team working so they can share information and time needs to be allocated for this to happen.

- *Time should be taken to reflect on different models of team working to ensure that best practice can be achieved.* Different settings have different models of team working with a variety of practitioners making up the team. Time needs to be taken to research and reflect on these models so that effective team working can be developed.

- *Effective team working develops over time.* Effective teams are ones that have been built up gradually over time with all team members contributing to and being a part of the process.

- *Team building and development are continuous and teams need to meet regularly.* Team working never stops and teams need time set aside to meet regularly in order to develop.

- *Time is needed for practitioners to observe and learn from one another.* Practitioners must respect, value and understand each other's practice and this can only be achieved through observation of one another's practice.

Key messages from Chapter 6 – Time to self-evaluate

- *How time is used in practice needs to be evaluated.* We have argued that time is not necessarily used effectively with young children. To ensure that it is, it must be evaluated. The evaluation framework (Tables 6.1–6.5) for this chapter enables teams to evaluate this area of their practice and develop effective ways of working.

- *Teams need to invest time in evaluation.* Evaluation takes time and teams must set aside time to conduct it.

- *Time needs to be taken to ensure that all members of the team are involved in evaluation.* Evaluation of time is a whole team process and time needs to be given to enable all team members to meet, have dialogue and reflect.

- *Effective evaluation involves reflection and action planning.* Evaluation is a cyclical process which involves reflecting on what has been evaluated and making plans for future action.

- *Evaluation is ongoing.* Evaluation never stops. Practice is continually changing and new ideas need to be incorporated and reflected upon. There is no end point as practice can always be improved.

Time and the Reggio Emilia approach to early years education

As outlined in the introduction to the Reggio Emilia approach the underpinning philosophy relies upon the continual reflection and discourse on the nature of childhood, children and learning. In addition, the child's world, including the home and the community, needs to be understood and incorporated into the life of the setting. This obviously involves time.

The use of time within this approach is referred to in each chapter. The curriculum comes from the children and time is spent on observing and reflecting on their ideas to inform planning. Time is spent on getting to know children and working with them at their own pace. The use of space ensures that time can be used in a variety of ways. Time is taken to document children's learning and development and this again informs practice. Parental partnership is integral to their way of working. This is taken further with the interaction of parents, children, staff and the wider community being at the heart of the philosophy. Time is allocated for serious, ongoing dialogue between staff and parents. Time is also spent on teamwork, especially on in-depth discussion so that children's and team members' learning is taken forward.

The Reggio Emilia way of working is one of constant reflection and evaluation. However, it is not a way of working that can be transported to another culture and educational environment. What we would hope is that, through this discussion, we have highlighted an approach that respects and understands the importance of time. When considering the use of time in your own settings, a great deal can be learned by becoming familiar with other approaches that really work. The Reggio Emilia approach will provide material for discussion and reflection.

Ultimately, we hope that *time* in the Foundation Stage may be used more effectively so that children and practitioners have at least some time to 'stand and stare'.

References

Abbott, L. and Nutbrown, C. (eds) (2001) *Experiencing Reggio Emilia: Implications for Pre-School Provision*. Buckingham: Open University Press.

Alexander, R. (2000) *Culture and Pedagogy*. Oxford: Blackwell.

Aubrey, C., David, T., Godfrey, R. and Thompson, L. (2000) *Early Childhood Educational Research*. London: RoutledgeFalmer.

BBC (1996) *The Nation's Favourite Poems*. London: BBC Books.

BBC (2004) *Learning Curve*. Radio 4, 13 July.

Bell, A. and Finch, S. (2004) *Sixth Survey of Parents of Three and Four Year Old Children and their Use of Early Years Services*. Nottingham: DfES Publications.

Blenkin, G. M. and Kelly, A. V. (1992) *Assessment in Early Childhood Education*. London: Paul Chapman Publishing.

Blenkin, G. M. and Kelly, A. V. (1996) *Assessment in Early Childhood Education* (2nd edn). London: Paul Chapman Publishing.

Blenkin, G. and Yue, N. (1994) 'Profiling early years practitioners: some first impressions from a national survey', *Early Years*, **15**(1), 13–22.

Boushel, M., Fawcett, M. and Selwyn, J. (2000) *Focus on Early Childhood*. Oxford: Blackwell Science.

Bruce, T. (1991) *Time to Play in Early Childhood*. London: Hodder & Stoughton.

Bruce, T. (1997) *Early Childhood Education*. London: Hodder & Stoughton.

Bruce, T. and Meggitt, C. (2002) *Child Care and Education*. London: Hodder & Stoughton.

CACE (Central Advisory Council for Education) (1966) *Children and Their Primary Schools* (the Plowden Report). London: HMSO.

Carr, M. (2001) *Assessment in Early Childhood Settings*. London: Paul Chapman Publishing.

Clark, A., McQuail, S. and Moss, P. (2003) *Exploring the Field of Listening to and Consulting with Young Children*. London: DfES Publications.

Clark, A. and Moss, P. (2001) *Listening to Young Children: The Mosaic Approach*. London: NCB.

Claxton, G. (1998) *Hare Brain Tortoise Mind*. London: Fourth Estate Ltd.

Cleave, S. and Brown, S. (1991) *Early to School: Four Year Olds in Infant Classes*. London: NFER/Routledge.

Cockburn, A. D. (2001) *Teaching Children 3 to 11: A Student Guide*. London: Paul Chapman Publishing.

Cousins, J. (1999) *Listening to Four Year Olds*. London: National Early Years Network.

David, T. (1999) *Young Children Learning*. London: Paul Chapman Publishing.

De Berker, J. (1999) 'Steiner education', lecture to PGCE students, Bath Spa University College.

Department for Education and Employment (1998) *The National Literacy Strategy*. London: DfEE.

Department for Education and Employment (1999) *The National Numeracy Strategy*. London: DfEE.

Department for Education and Employment (2000) *Guidance on the Organisation of the NLS in Reception Classes*. London: DfEE.

Department for Education and Science (1990) *Starting with Quality. The Report of the Committee of Inquiry into the Quality of the Educational Experience offered to 3- and 4-year-olds, chaired by Angela Rumbold CBE MP*. London: HMSO.

Department for Education and Skills (2004) *Provision for Children under Five Years of Age in England January 2004 (Provisional)*. Available on: http://www.dfes.gov.uk/rsgateway/DB/SFR/s000363/SFR15–2004pdf (accessed 29 May 2004).

Department for Education and Skills/Department for Work and Pensions (2002) *Sure Start*. Nottingham: DfES Publications.

Department for Education and Skills/Teacher Training Agency (2002) *Qualifying to Teach*. London: TTA.

Desforges, C. and Abouchaar, A. (2003) *The Impact of Parental Involvement, Parental Support and Family Education on Pupil Achievement and Adjustment: A Literature Review* (Research Report RR433). London: DfES Publications.

Devereux, J. and Miller, L. (2003) *Working with Children in the Early Years*. London: David Fulton Publishers.

Donaldson, M. (1978) *Children's Minds*. Glasgow: Collins.

Dowling, M. (1992) *Education 3–5*. London: Paul Chapman Publishing.

Dowling, M. (1995) *Starting School at Four: A Joint Endeavour*. London: Paul Chapman Publishing.

Downie, A. and McNeish, D. (2000) *Evaluation Toolkit: A Practical Guide to Project Evaluation*. Leeds Health Action Zone and Barnardo's.

Drake, J. (2001) *Planning Children's Play and Learning in the Foundation Stage*. London: David Fulton.

Drummond, M. J. (1994) *Assessing Children's Learning*. London: David Fulton.

Edwards, C., Gandini, L. and Forman, G. (1998) *The Hundred Languages of Children: The Reggio Emilia Approach – Advanced Reflections*. Greenwood, CT: Ablex Publishing Corporation.

Fisher, J. (1996) *Starting from the Child*. Buckingham: Open University Press.

Fisher, J. (2002a) *Starting from the Child* (2nd edn). Buckingham: Open University Press.

Fisher, J. (2002b) *The Foundations of Learning*. Buckingham: Open University Press.

Fisher, R. (2000) 'Developmentally appropriate practice and a National Literacy Strategy'. *British Journal of Educational Studies*, **48**(1): 58–69.

Hohman, M. and Weikart, D. P. (1995) *Educating Young Children*. Michigan: High/Scope Press.

Hurst, J. and Joseph, J. (1998) *Supporting Early Learning: The Way Forward*. Buckingham: Open University Press.

Klein, R. (2000) 'Why sitting still for long periods can lead to poor posture in children', *TES*, 25 February.

Laevers, F., Vandenbussche, E., Kog, M. and Depondt, L. (1994) *A Process-Oriented Child Monitoring System for Young Children*. Leuven: Centre for Experiential Education, Catholic University of Leuven.

Lee, J. (2004) 'In need of parent skills', *TES*, 16 July.

Lyus, V. (1998) *Management in the Early Years*. London: Hodder & Stoughton.

McInnes, K. (2001) 'What is the educational reality for four-year-olds?' unpublished MA Dissertation, Bath Spa University College.

Melhuish, E., Sylva, K., Sammons, P., Siraj-Blatchford, I. and Taggart, B. (2001) *Social, Behavioural and Cognitive Development at 3–4 years in Relation to Family Background: The Effective Provision of Pre-School Education, EPPE Project*. (Technical paper 7) London: The Institute of Education.

Ministry of Education (1996) *Te Whariki: He Whariki Matauranga mo nga Mokopuna o Aotearoa: Early Childhood Curriculum*. Wellington: Learning Media.

Moyles, J. (1992) *Organising for Learning in the Primary Classroom*. Buckingham: Open University Press.

Moyles, J. (ed.) (1995) *Beginning Teaching, Beginning Learning*. Buckingham: Open University Press.

Ofsted (1993) *First Class: The Standards and Quality of Education in Reception Classes*. London: HMSO.

Ofsted (2000) *The National Literacy Strategy: The Second Year*. London: Ofsted Publications Centre.

Ofsted (2004a) *Transition from the Reception Year to Year 1: An Evaluation by HMI*. London: Ofsted Publications Centre.

Ofsted (2004b) 'Children at the centre: an evaluation of early excellence centres', HMI 2222. Available on www.ofsted.gov.uk/publications.

Parry, M. and Archer, H. (1975) *Handbook for Students and Teachers: Two to Five*. London: Macmillan Education.

Pascal, C., Bertram, A., Ramsden, F., Georgesen, J., Saunders, M. and Mould, C. (1996) *Evaluating and Developing Quality in Early Childhood Settings*. Worcester: WCHE.

Pascal, C. and Bertram, T. (1997) *Effective Early Learning. Case Studies in Improvement*. London: Hodder & Stoughton.

Pugh, G. (1996) 'Four-year-olds in school: what is appropriate provision?' *NCB*, October/Winter.

Qualifications and Curriculum Authority (QCA) (2000) *The Curriculum Guidance for the Foundation Stage*. London: DfEE.

Qualifications and Curriculum Authority (QCA) (2001) *Planning for Learning in the Foundation Stage*. London: DfES.

Qualifications and Curriculum Authority (QCA) (2003) *Foundation Stage Profile*. London: DfES.

Rodd, J. (1984) *Leadership in Early Childhood Services: The Pathway to Professionalism*. Buckingham: Open University Press.

School Curriculum and Assessment Authority (SCAA) (1996) *Nursery Education: Desirable Outcomes for Children's Learning on Entering Compulsory Education*. London: DfEE.

Sharp, C. (2002) *School Starting Age: European Policy and Recent Research*. Swindon: National Foundation for Educational Research.

Siraj-Blatchford, I. and Siraj-Blatchford, J. (2001) 'A content analysis of pedagogy in the DfEE/QCA 2000 Guidance', *Early Education*, 5, Autumn.

Siraj-Blatchford, I., Sylva, K., Muttock, S., Gilden, R. and Bell, D. (2002) *Researching Effective Pedagogy in the Early Years*. Nottingham: DfES.

Soler, J. and Miller, L. (2003) 'The struggle for early childhood curricula: a comparison of the English Foundation Stage Curriculum, Te Whariki and Reggio Emilia', *International Journal of Early Years Education*, 11(1), 57–67.

Staggs, L. (2000) 'Curriculum guidance for the early years', *Early Years Educator*, 2(6): 21–3.

Sure Start (2004) www.surestart.gov.uk/aboutsurestart/makingsurestartwork2 (accessed 29 July). See also www.ness.bbk.ac.uk

Sylva, K., Melhuish, E., Sammons, P., Siraj-Blatchford, I. and Taggart, B. (2004) *The Effective Provision of Pre-School Education (EPPE) Project: Findings from Pre-School to End of Key Stage 1*. Nottingham: DfES Publications.

Sylva, K., Sammons, P., Melhuish, E., Siraj-Blatchford, I. and Taggart, B. (1997–2003) *The Effective Provision of Pre-School Education (EPPE) Project*. London: The Institute of Education, University of London.

Tizard, B. and Hughes, M. (1984) *Young Children Learning*. London: Fontana Press.

Wells, G. (1996) *The Meaning Makers*. London: Hodder & Stoughton.

Whalley, M. (1994) *Learning to Be Strong: Integrating Education and Care in Early Childhood*. London: Hodder & Stoughton.

Whalley, M. (2001) *Involving Parents in their Children's Learning*. London: Paul Chapman Publishing.

Whitebread, D. (ed.) (1996) *Teaching and Learning in the Early Years*. London: Routledge.

Whitebread, D. (2000) *The Psychology of Teaching*. London: Routledge Falmer.

Whitehead, M. (1999) *Supporting Language and Literacy Development in the Early Years*. Buckingham: Open University Press.

Williams, J. (2003) *Promoting Independent Learning in the Primary Classroom*. Buckingham: Open University Press.

Wolfendale. S. (ed.) (1989) *Parental Involvement. Developing Networks between School, Home and Community*. London: Cassell.

Wood, D. (1988) *How Children Think and Learn*. Oxford: Blackwell.

Woodhead, M. (1989) ' "School starts at five . . . or four years old?" The rationale for changing admission policies in England and Wales', *Journal of Education Policy*, 4(1): 1–21.

Wragg, T. (2003) 'Reception regime gives staff 3,510 boxes to tick', www.tes.co.uk/search/search_display.asp?section=archive&sub_section=News+%26+opinion&id=37387 &Type=0 (accessed 19 July 2004).

Index